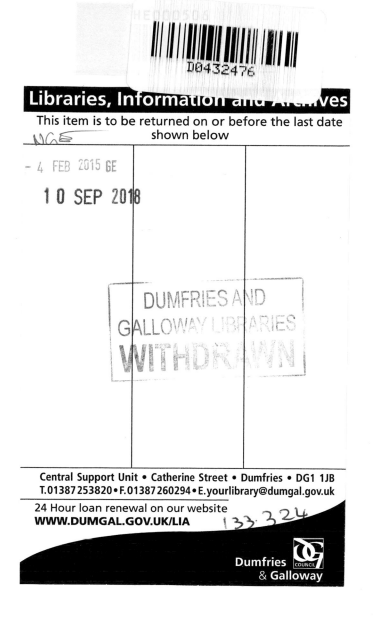

THE TAROT MASTERS

THE TAROT MASTERS

Insights from the World's Leading Tarot Experts

EDITED BY
KIM ARNOLD

HAY HOUSE

Carlsbad, California • New York City • London • Sydney
Johannesburg • Vancouver • Hong Kong • New Delhi

First published and distributed in the United Kingdom by:
Hay House UK Ltd, Astley House, 33 Notting Hill Gate, London W11 3JQ
Tel: +44 (0)20 3675 2450; Fax: +44 (0)20 3675 2451; www.hayhouse.co.uk

Published and distributed in the United States of America by:
Hay House Inc., PO Box 5100, Carlsbad, CA 92018-5100
Tel: (1) 760 431 7695 or (800) 654 5126; Fax: (1) 760 431 6948 or (800) 650 5115
www.hayhouse.com

Published and distributed in Australia by:
Hay House Australia Ltd, 18/36 Ralph St, Alexandria NSW 2015
Tel: (61) 2 9669 4299; Fax: (61) 2 9669 4144; www.hayhouse.com.au

Published and distributed in the Republic of South Africa by:
Hay House SA (Pty) Ltd, PO Box 990, Witkoppen 2068
Tel/Fax: (27) 11 467 8904; www.hayhouse.co.za

Published and distributed in India by:
Hay House Publishers India, Muskaan Complex, Plot No.3, B-2,
Vasant Kunj, New Delhi 110 070; Tel: (91) 11 4176 1620; Fax: (91) 11 4176 1630
www.hayhouse.co.in

Distributed in Canada by:
Ra... St, Vancouver BC V6P 6E5
...Fax: (1) 604 323 2600

© Kim Arnold, 2013

A catalogue record for this book is available from the British Library.

ISBN 978-1-78180-304-2

Tarot card artwork created by Kati Oppermann

Printed and bound in Great Britain by TJ International, Padstow, Cornwall.

MIX
Paper from
responsible sources
FSC
www.fsc.org   FSC® C013056

CONTENTS

Part Two: More Tarot Masters

The Contributors 146

ACKNOWLEDGEMENTS

First and foremost, thank you to everyone who has contributed to this book.

To Melanie Young, Diane Ebeck, Geraldine and Bali Beskin for their continued loyalty, support, encouragement and help with the UK Tarot Conference, without which this book would not exist.

To Lyn Howarth-Olds, whose *Letters to the Past* Tarot project inspired this one, thank you for the time spent, along with Leanne McGregor, editing these pages.

Heartfelt thanks to my family, who have supported and encouraged me in every way possible; especially my husband Martin who pushed me when I doubted myself – Martin, your continued support keeps me sane.

I would also like to acknowledge Jonathan Dee and Hermann Haindl, both of whom were speakers at our 2010 Conference and have since sadly departed this world. Both were kind and special souls who contributed so much to Tarot.

INTRODUCTION

O ver the last decade, there has been a huge shift in attitude towards Tarot, and thankfully it has been mostly for the better.

The 38 contributors to this book have all played a part in bringing Tarot out of the suburbs and into the mainstream, and I am thrilled that they have agreed to take part in this collaborative project.

Being curious as to what makes someone pick up a deck of Tarot cards for the first time, I asked the contributors the following questions: How did your Tarot journey begin and what inspired you? What is your interpretation of a Major Arcana card, and what is it about the card that you either love or loathe? Their responses can be read on the pages that follow.

My hope is that this collection of work will become a legacy and inspire future generations of Tarot enthusiasts. Just imagine if we had such a book with contributions from Waite, Colman Smith and the like!

PART ONE

THE
MAJOR
ARCANA

INTRODUCTION

$\sim\!\!\infty\!\!\sim$

As a Tarot reader and teacher, I often associate people with the traits of the Major Arcana Tarot cards. Expanding on this idea, I have personally chosen 22 influential authors, artists and teachers of Tarot to represent each of the cards in the Major Arcana.

If you look closely at each card you will see the contributor's initials, discreetly placed within the design of the card that has been 'assigned' to them. In some cases, the connection between the person and the card will be obvious; in others, the connection may be a little more obscure.

I have my own reasons for each association – maybe I will reveal all in the next book!

$\sim$

O

The Fool

0

THE FOOL

with Kim Arnold

The first card of Tarot: The Fool, numbered zero. A new journey is about to begin. Where will that journey take us? Are we about to abandon what we know to be safe and secure?

There is an element of risk-taking with this card, although the message reminds us that we have free will.

The Fool has great faith but tends to look only at the positive aspects of what lies ahead. Just make sure you weigh up the pros and cons before you leap into the unknown! Often, The Fool appears in a reading when the querent is ready for change.

For me, the main aspect of The Fool is that the road ahead is full of potential and invites change. However, the way we handle that change dictates whether the experience will be positive or negative.

Kim Arnold talks Tarot

From early childhood I always felt there was more to life than just existing and I had a fascination for all things magical.

I was 17 when I attended my first clairvoyant evening. I was sitting in the front row – strange in itself as I was painfully shy – and during the medium's address, she handed me her ring and announced to the audience that I was going to demonstrate psychometry! Mortified and embarrassed, I took the ring and closed my eyes. In my mind's eye, I was in a house where scenes were being played out to me in great detail. I relayed what I saw. At the end of the evening, the medium told me everything I had said was true, and invited me to study at the Spiritualist Association of Great Britain. At the time I thought that if you conjured up spirits they would follow you home, so I graciously declined.

'How about Tarot?' she said. 'If you don't like it you can pop the cards back in the box and forget about them.' Now she had my attention. A trip to Mysteries in Covent Garden to purchase the IJJ Swiss deck followed, and the rest – as they say – is history.

The Magician

I

THE MAGICIAN

with Ina Cüsters-van Bergen

Come with me on an inner journey. The road starts in darkness, so ignite the light of the Spirit and it will shine.

Follow me as I lead you into the sanctuary of the Temple of Life: a path that has been walked by generations of sages, leading you to eternal patterns of inner growth. I conjure up a magical wand. Take it and draw the symbol of eternity above your head.

Freeze in this position for a minute – you will become the Hebrew letter aleph: realize that divinity breathes through you! But why then is The Magician connected with the Hebrew letter beth?

Follow me over the path of black and white tiles: the Path of Life takes you through darkness and light. Both are necessary for growth. Work with the opportunities life offers you. Transcend them on the altar standing amidst your Inner Temple.

Why do you need an altar? Shaped like the Cube of Space, it helps you to orientate yourself: thus you can work with the divine forces surrounding you.

More magical instruments start to appear. First, a wand. You have already used one to connect yourself to eternity. But this wand is special: it is the magical wand of Mercury, the caduceus. With it you travel between Heaven and Earth. It is the key to the development of your spirit. It fits exactly on the Tree of Life. Use this wand and develop magical powers.

A chalice is filled with the waters of life. Look into it and find the scrying mirror: revealing truth in your life, developing your inner sight and psychic powers. Drink from it and you will find the Grail.

Now a sword appears: made from pure spiritual light, forged from a golden ray of the Sun. Use it to protect the light in your life.

My next gift is a platter, round like the Earth herself. Inscribed on it is the pentagram, for it is your key to the elements of the wise – air, water, fire, earth and spirit – brought into a perfect balance.

Work with these magical tools and with the elements of the wise, and your life will change into the blessed House for the Spirit. This is why The Magician is connected with the letter beth.

May your garden be full of lilies and may you be nurtured by the mystical rose.

Ina Cüsters-van Bergen talks Tarot

My journey with Tarot started as a teenager. During my investigations to discover the world, I found my first pack of Tarot cards in the trendy centre De Kosmos in Amsterdam, and I fell in love with the Book of Thoth. I still use my first deck; for me the beauty of the paintings and the depth of the symbolism have never been surpassed by any other.

Fascinated by questions about love and everyday issues, I started using the cards. But something in the trumps triggered me to look deeper. A mystery was hidden just around the corner and I tried to find out what it was, only to discover that the cards opened the way to even greater mysteries. I worked with the cards from my 17th year on, and I am still learning from them. Tarot gives access to the Matrix of Life.

I started to use the cards to find answers to questions about myself, and situations that puzzled me. Unexpectedly, new and hidden depths started to surface from the cards. Tarot became a highway to the inner planes, and to the mysterious powers of – magic! I discovered that when working with a card, the trump triggered events to happen in my life. I suddenly faced challenges that caused me to grow spiritually and as a person. I contacted entities that appeared as inner plane teachers, showing the highways towards the higher mind. They started to explain to me the secrets of consciousness: my real adventure had now begun!

Tarot now answered highly philosophical questions, enabled me to delve deep into my subconscious mind, and uncovered hidden wisdom. Excited by my experiences, I started to investigate the relationship between Tarot and Kabbalah. I experimented with them in relation to the Egyptian underworld books.

Now the cards became real magical tools. The outcome was so spectacular that I wanted to share my results with other people, so I wrote a course of 50 lessons combining Kabbalah, Tarot, magical exercises and mythology. This course is now the basic training of the Hermetic Order of the Temple of Starlight.

My Tarot journey has been a life-changing experience, as it is for everyone who uses Tarot as doorways to inner wisdom.

~

II

The Priestess

II

THE PRIESTESS

with Mary K. Greer

In the Waite Smith Tarot, The High Priestess card shows a Moon-crowned, blue-robed woman; a priestess sitting between black and white pillars in front of a veil decorated with palm trees and pomegranates. For A.E. Waite, she was the mystical presence of the divine in humankind, the love aspect in deity, the Moon, whose light comes from the eternal. On Earth, she is the secret church, the highest sense of the mysteries. She sits concealed at the Portal of Atziluth, between the Pillars of the Eternal Temple, with the Book of the Secret Law open on her knees. As crown of the middle pillar, she is the ladder by which all souls ascend and descend; all duality is finally united in her. Source of oracles, the holy soul, she reads all that is written in the Book of the Mysteries.

The Priestess card graphically depicts a woman's sexuality as a hidden sanctuary, telling us that the mysteries of sex are sacred. The Priestess is profound feminine wisdom: an inner truth that lies behind outer signs, symbols or events. She is mysterious, wise and virginal – meaning 'whole' or 'belonging to herself'. She mediates between the conscious and unconscious, between our outer and inner worlds. Her insights are not given in words but in subtle impressions, dreams or metaphoric images and feelings – for these are her language. As the Moon reflects the light of the Sun, so she mirrors the inner self of others. She counsels spending time alone, withdrawing into solitude, paying attention to the natural rhythms and cycles of the body and of nature. Honouring feelings and intuitions over reason, she offers guidance and understanding in the form of impressions and dreams. Open yourself to the Priestess, for, through her, you access the deeper significance, spiritual purpose, values and principles that give greater meaning to your life and work.

For me, she is my teacher, my guide, my soul; magnetic yet untouchable, alluring yet perpetually serene, empathic yet forever veiled and unknowable; she is myself, and more than I can ever be.

Mary K. Greer talks Tarot

My Tarot journey began well over 40 years ago. Like many of my generation, I first saw Tarot cards on a daytime soap opera called *Dark Shadows*, which screened just as I got home from school. Later, while in college, my best friend got Eden Gray's *Tarot Revealed* for Christmas. I became fascinated by the images of the cards in the book and intrigued by what they could reveal about a person, so I asked everyone where I might find a Tarot deck. Learning of a metaphysical bookstore on the other side of Tampa, Florida, I borrowed a car and went on what I consider my first spiritual quest – to find a Tarot deck.

I discovered not only the cards, but the whole world of esotericism. Within a year I decided I would teach Tarot in college and someday write a book on the subject; it was the impetus for me to continue on to get my Master's degree.

As an English and Theatre Arts major, another thing that drew me to Tarot was a fascination with symbolism. I had just begun what became a lifelong study of Jungian archetypes and psychology, along with Joseph Campbell's hero's journey. I realized that the stories I saw in the cards were metaphors for what was happening in someone's life.

In 1970, after college, I spent a year in London, where I learned astrology and dated a man who worked at The Atlantis Bookshop, giving me access to London's occult underground.

Returning to the USA, I taught Tarot at two colleges, including the New College of California in San Francisco. As well as my teaching role, I was director of advising, and designer of a degree-completion programme. This involved evaluating one's professional and life development in journal format.

A major breakthrough came when I realized that while all the books of the time said not to read Tarot for yourself, everyone I knew did. And so I brought all my interests together, and this resulted in my first book, *Tarot for Yourself*. The idea was birthed at the same time as my daughter, while I was on a year's sabbatical in Mexico.

III

The Empress

III

THE EMPRESS

with Caitlín Matthews

We can trace the limitless abundance of this card from the Celtic Triple Mothers – who were depicted bearing babies, fruit, grain and bread in their laps, and who were once venerated throughout Europe – to the courtly, medieval empresses whose matronage fuelled the arts, relieved poverty and endowed hospitals, colleges and monasteries.

The Empress oversees the fertility of the land and the life of its plants, animals and people. She represents the guardianship of the earth, maintaining a loving watch over all life, imbuing it with her instinct or mother-wit – the basic common sense by which we are protected and sustained. Her essential self-respect lends grace and dignity to every living being, encouraging us to nourish our innate skills and gifts so that we may also be a source of delight to those around us. This quality of total immersion and commitment to our lives is what shapes our personhood, our sexuality and our delight in life itself. Whatever blessings we deliver during our lifetime, The Empress urges us to be generous and share them within our community, so that all might flourish.

Upright, The Empress can represent abundance, nourishment, wealth of resources, fulfilment, reverence for life, the earth, community-mindedness, motherhood, fertility, sexuality, loving guardianship, value, grace, dignity, honour, health, wholeness and emotional growth.

Reversed, The Empress can represent infertility, poverty, delay in accomplishment, the squandering of or the inability to share resources, inertia or laziness, emotional immaturity, self-neglect or self-immersion.

Caitlín Matthews talks Tarot

I grew up in a house with no books and few toys, subjected to long, aching periods of boredom – a time highly conducive to the development of the imagination I now appreciate. The main companions of my lonely hours were a box of chessmen and a pack of playing cards, which I used as playthings with their own identities.

In the cards: the dark-haired courts of the suit of spades held a more royal authority for me than the fair-haired hearts and diamonds, while the suit of clubs emanated a kind of performer's pizzazz. The Queen of Diamonds was the heroine; the Jacks were roguish and louche, except for the Jack of Spades who was a steady sort of chap. The King of Diamonds was an influential man about town.

The pip cards wove their own patterns, lining up in dances and quadrilles, weaving the power of their face values into my stories. Sometimes, the court cards would be trains running along the lines of the pip cards. Other times, the pip cards would make houses and palaces for the courts to live in. Stories spilled out of the cards.

I bought my first Tarot pack, a Grimaud Marseilles, from Foyles bookshop in London. The cards had simple primary colours so the effect was very striking. I found I couldn't use them late at night or they would be indelibly imprinted upon my retina and would show up in my dreams.

I owned an Eden Gray Tarot book, but my reading skills really picked up when I received lessons from an itinerant man who used the Waite Smith Tarot intuitively, reading from the pictures alone. He read little signs in the cards, just as the Roma people leave patrins or roadside patterns of stones and twigs for other travellers to follow. I am grateful to him for that teaching.

Then I came across the Man, Myth and Magic series of magazines and understood that I could actually enter the cards, not just in meditation but also during readings, which I've done ever since. Coming full circle, I'm now studying playing cards as cartomancy and those early games I played are proving valuable as I develop new skills.

⁓

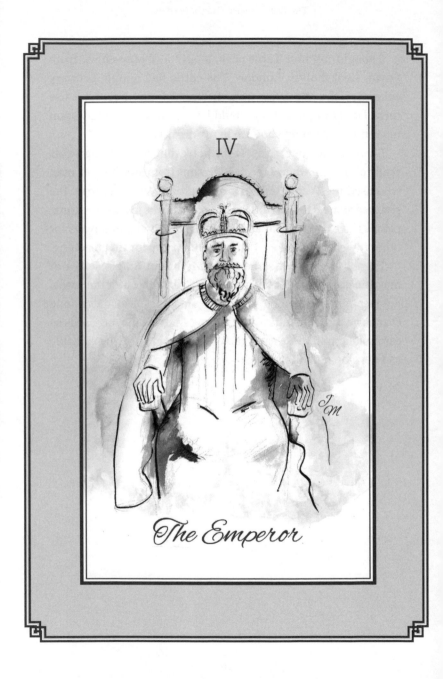

IV

THE EMPEROR

with John Matthews

To me, The Emperor oversees all life with courage and vision, stability and commitment. He is the Green Man, King Arthur, the Emperor of Rome and the god of change and fecundity. He defines and defends his realm with humanity, wielding authority with responsibility. His strength becomes a point of stability for others, establishing clear structures and helpful boundaries. His is the virility and energy that powers the tasks we undertake; that drives greenness out of the earth. He enables us to take the lead and get organized, to follow a regime, to hit schedules responsibly and maintain the highest standards. When we take up our space in life with courage, The Emperor ensures that we possess natural authority and hold the boundaries without wavering.

The Emperor encourages qualities that enable us to turn ideas into reality, lead the field or bring plans to fruition. He can help create a secure environment that gives protection to others. The Emperor is present when responsible love or fatherhood leads – in the workplace, the family or the environment. Authoritative energy and delight in potency bring organization; authenticity emerges from taking up his challenge.

In its negative aspect, this card can indicate a censorious attitude or overly rigid structure that prescribes the boundaries of life. Indecisiveness or sitting on the fence mean that others have to do our work, and failure to lead leaves things in disarray. At its lowest ebb this leads to arrogance or perfectionism, even megalomania or delusions of grandeur that can overwhelm common sense. We need to take care that fatherly qualities don't become too overwhelming, and try to avoid spending too much time jockeying for position, otherwise we may find ourselves immersed in competition for its own sake.

Overall this card can be said to represent all that is best and most positive about masculinity – when it is balanced, even-handed and kindly, as well as strong, durable and true. This is often achieved through the balancing energy of The Empress, without whom The Emperor may become monolithic.

John Matthews talks Tarot

I'm not sure when I first became aware of Tarot. Growing up in the 60s, I flirted with everything and remember buying a copy of *The Mythic Tarot* by Liz Greene, which I liked but found did not work the way I wanted it to.

My wife, Caitlín, and I started working on *The Western Way*, a study of the history of the esoteric and the mystical, and began seriously researching Tarot. I found it raised as many questions as it answered. Where had these images come from? No one seemed to agree.

Caitlín and I had been discussing things, bouncing ideas off each other, and one of us – or maybe both at the same moment – said: 'What would an Arthurian Tarot look like?' We explored both the legends of Arthur and the images of Tarot and found they fitted so well together. We began working on a deck with artist Miranda Gray. In creating it we learned a huge amount about Tarot. The deck is still in print.

Since then Caitlín and I have created eight new Tarot decks between us, and each time we learn more. I find as the years pass – and I have spent more and more time working with Tarot – I'm still amazed by the wealth of wisdom and power these images possess.

I still go back to the question I asked long ago: where did the images come from? I don't think they are from ancient Egypt or Atlantis or Mars, but I do think they speak to us from a time when there were no words and we thought in images. We can still learn more today from these archetypes than we can from reading a million words.

❦

V

THE HIEROPHANT

with Mark Ryan

In The Wildwood Tarot, the archetype usually known as The Hierophant is called The Ancestor. She stands for ancient memory, the spirit of nature in the subconscious human psyche, and the call of the wild. An antlered figure, clad in reindeer skins and evergreen leaves, stands at the gateway to the Wildwood, framed by silver birch trees. The Ancestor greets you as you walk up the path that leads into the forest.

She is a creature of myth – half-animal, half-human – linked to the part of our soul that is most ancient and most closely related to the natural world. She is a guardian of the sacred spirit of the land and summons you by beating the drum to the heartbeat of the Earth. There is a part of you at work here that unconsciously heard this drumbeat and felt the first desire to walk the path. It is the overpowering strength and patience of nature. It is the awesome and relentless turning of the cycle that brings spring and warmth, an end to hibernation and the reawakening of abundant life.

Thus you make the leap and start a new cycle. Your instinctive spirit has felt it necessary to lead you to the gateway and a new path. You may have been reluctant or concerned at first, but whether you realize it or not, a shift has occurred. You may feel wary of the unknown denizens that await you in the forest, but the ancient Ancestor within will guide and reassure you as you greet new experiences on the path.

Trust your inner voice. Listen to your own instinctive and inquisitive nature. Your inner ancestor is strong, patient and wise. Let him or her draw you on to the forest adventure with new eyes and a joyful heart.

Mark Ryan talks Tarot

As a boy growing up in Yorkshire, I spent many happy Sunday afternoons playing in Sherwood Forest, and during this time my love of the Robin Hood stories was born. Maybe the seeds of my interest in Tarot were planted too, though they didn't sprout until quite a few years later.

I bought my first Tarot deck sometime in the late 70s, but found we didn't get along. Something about the structure didn't work for me.

Somewhere around 1991, I was discussing Tarot ideas with artist Chesca Potter. By this time I had been working on the TV show *Robin of Sherwood* – playing the part of Nazir the Saracen – and my head was full of woodland imagery. Together we laid out the Major Arcana of a Rider Waite Tarot and organized it around the Wheel of the Year, a seasonal pattern that acknowledges the archetypal beings who live in the woods. Chesca and I talked for hours, exploring what a Tarot deck based on these primal archetypes might look like.

Thus The Greenwood Tarot was born. It developed a cult following, but eventually went out of print. For the next 20 years I was asked if it would ever be available again. Then John Matthews approached me about developing the original book and deck into something new. We took the concept to Eddison Sadd, who had seen the original Greenwood Tarot years ago. They too loved the idea, and with new artist Will Worthington on board, we began work on The Wildwood Tarot – the original name of The Greenwood Tarot.

One of the things I wanted with this new deck – and that Will achieved brilliantly – was to make the artwork accessible. There's no specific era, and most of the characters look like real people. We wanted to keep the timelessness of it because the primordial concepts go back to man's first steps on the face of the planet. The drive of the pack, which must drive the art, is that it's going back to man's first conceptualization of art.

There are a lot of influences at work in Tarot, but I've always believed the magic is in your head. Whether you believe that the universe has a consciousness of its own, or whether you believe there is some divine entity, there's a part of the human conscious and subconscious mind that can transcend that.

There are at least three elements interacting when you read the cards: the reader, the artwork itself, and that little spark of magic that gets conveyed through consciousness and language. This to me is the definition of magic – the magic of Tarot.

~

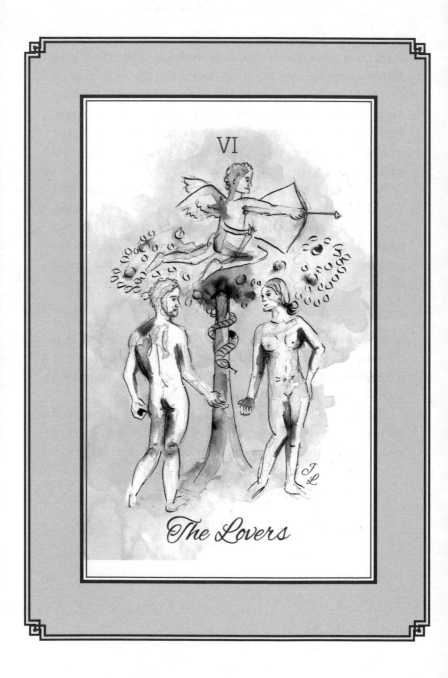

VI

THE LOVERS

with Jane Lyle

The Lovers card is as complex and meaningful as love itself. The design of this card varies considerably from one deck to another, revealing the different ways people have tried to show us its essence. In some old decks, such as the Marseilles, a young man is shown with two women – one younger, one older. Cupid hovers above them, aiming his arrows of desire at the human beings below. The older woman is sometimes shown in the role of priestess, about to join the young couple in marriage. In other designs, the man stands between the two women – perhaps his mother and his lover – having to choose between them. The choice is actually between security and familiarity, and the adventure and risk represented by a new love relationship.

In the Rider Waite deck, Arthur Edward Waite altered the old designs to show Adam and Eve in the Garden of Eden with the archangel Raphael above them. Adam stands in front of the Tree of Life and looks towards Eve, who stands in front of the Tree of Knowledge gazing up at the angel. Adam symbolizes the rational, conscious mind. He can only become aware of the angel – his higher self or super-conscious – through his union with Eve, who represents the unconscious.

Traditionally, The Lovers shows that love and choice are connected and this can manifest in a number of ways. An important love relationship is the most obvious interpretation, and very often this is the case. The choice here is to get involved, to make a commitment and to take on the responsibility of a serious relationship. Accompanying cards will clarify and confirm this meaning. Sometimes, just to complicate things further, there will be a choice of potential partners.

At other times, The Lovers can mean working towards an inner marriage – creating a union of opposing elements in the personality, resulting in a sense of inner balance and harmony. This is reflected in the journey of Tarot itself, as the naïve, innocent Fool encounters trials, challenges and lessons on the way to journey's end at The World. As the journey proceeds, the conscious and unconscious learn how to work together to connect with the higher self and receive divine wisdom.

The idea of choice also manifests when someone feels uncertain about his or her circumstance or relationship. We can choose to continue with what is familiar, or to stretch out, take a risk and try something new. To discover what is in our hearts we must use our intuition, meditate, and ask the higher self for guidance. There is no stark right or wrong answer; the truth – as always – lies within.

Jane Lyle talks Tarot

In many ways my fascination with Tarot was inevitable – it sprang straight out of my family background. I was fortunate to grow up with open-minded people who loved to talk about anything and everything. I was psychic from a very early age, and thankfully this was treated as completely natural. I learned to read tea leaves with my grandmother and, later on, how to read playing cards. When I was about 13, my mother gave me a Marseilles Tarot deck. A Rider Waite Smith deck soon followed, as did the search for Tarot books to guide me through the wealth of symbolism and dreamlike images I loved.

My first-ever Tarot book was *The Tarot Revealed* by Eden Gray. I still believe this work is a wonderful introduction to the world of Tarot and treasure the author's wise words. Her advice was to stress the positive, to encourage self-development, and to realize how the guidance offered by a spread of cards could 'plant seeds' that would bloom later. Thanks to Eden Gray, I also discovered the practice of meditating on a particular card's image and noting the intuitions that arose from it. I still think this is an excellent way to get to know the Major Arcana, and it is something you can do at any time to tune in to a particular energy or archetype.

I came to understand that this mysterious deck of cards has many layers, and that its images and symbols appear in art and design from all over the world. I'm still delighted when I spot a picture or read a poem that resonates with Tarot's amazing collection of images and the profound meanings the cards carry.

For me, it is impossible to imagine a time when I will stop learning and discovering more about the cards. This is the true magic embodied in Tarot.

Tarot depicts the soul's journey – from The Fool to The World – and this journey is made many times and in many ways throughout our lives. Each time we meet a new set of experiences; we begin at a place where we know little about what lies ahead. Yet Tarot is always there, acting as a wise guide, a map, and an invaluable companion along the way.

⌐

VII

THE CHARIOT

with Richard Abbot

Major Arcanum show crossroads, turning points and life lessons. Lessons that we must all learn, sooner or later. In this sense I treat Tarot as a compendium of life skills, keys to a better life. With the Majors particularly, the issue is not what happens but how we react to what happens. The Chariot is an exemplar of this, fundamentally representing controlled forward momentum. Life is partly linear, if not entirely so, and The Chariot shows the need for a goal and a direction. The two animals, reins and two wheels that are often pictured in the card, show the need for you – the Charioteer – to gain awareness and control over the contrariness of your nature. We must all face and deal with obstacles. We must find a path and stick to it. We must begin a task and finish it, despite the many distractions and bumps in the road.

The Charioteer moves forward through personal effort. He is in the driver's seat, alone. He makes progress through understanding the numerology of seven.

Seven is about the mind and the heart, the inner self as opposed to the outer. The seven-type person is reflective, thoughtful and takes time over decisions, but once the matter is settled internally it is all systems go in the outer world. A successful Charioteer embodies this and knows that 'thought without action brings frustration, and action without thought brings disappointment.' He knows that all journeys need preparation, and as such the Charioteer is centred, calm, focused and still. This approach allows him to drive the Chariot at full speed without fear.

What happens when The Chariot is reversed? Literally, we see the wheels coming off. Failure – probably at the last moment – to succeed. The sudden collapse of plans and projects. A failure to plan is a plan to fail. And in the most mundane fashion, the car breaks down, the flight is cancelled and fallen leaves on the line stop the train getting through.

I have enjoyed a life closely involved with The Chariot, and I have learned that all journeys need breaks. No one can keep moving forward incessantly. The Chariot sometimes needs to be rested.

Richard Abbot talks Tarot

The year was 1989 and I had just started sixth form. Flicking through the local paper I noticed an ad for a psychic fayre at a local hotel, so I trotted along, ignorant but intrigued. After navigating my way past crystals and Scientologists, I found that through a strange twist of fate, someone I had booked a reading with no longer had space for me, so I sat down for 'some Tarot' with an older gentleman named Arthur. The tape recorder whirred away as he laid the cards down on the table with metronome-like timing.

Thwack went the cardboard as a series of remarkable coloured images appeared on the table before us. I later learned these came from the Morgan Greer Tarot.

As each card was laid out Arthur spoke, his voice measured and sure. I was enthralled by what I was hearing.

'Money worries, a need to take care of the pennies, to be frugal,' he said.

Damn right, I thought!

'A woman, blonde and slim, friendly though not romantic. She will become a lifelong friend.'

Oh, that sounds good.

Arthur continued on, describing the coming twelve months in great detail. 'Employment, new responsibilities, an unfamiliar environment at first, but one that you will master,' he said, snapping down the card for May 1990.

That can't be right, I thought, I am studying for my A-Levels, then going to university. I was still intrigued but now started to have doubts, as his predictions seemed more and more unlikely.

As quickly as I had sat down, I got up again with a tape of the session in hand.

'Stay in touch,' Arthur said as he wished me farewell.

Fast forward to spring, some three to four months later. Over the Christmas period I had got into all sorts of trouble. In hindsight I was lucky to be alive. Suffice to say, life had taken a turn for the worse, culminating in me being expelled from sixth form. I still lived at home with my parents and I was totally lost, bereft of the self-confidence I had six months earlier.

At rest in my room, I happened upon the recording of Arthur's reading. As I played the tape and heard the snap of the cards, I was instantly transported back to that day. I now heard Arthur's words with different ears and recalled the cards with new eyes. To my amazement everything that had been predicted had come true. I even heard words on the tape that I didn't remember hearing the first time round.

'December, Christmas, New Year – overindulgence, arrogance, carelessness – you must curb all these things if you are to avoid danger.' Arthur continued, 'January – rest, recovery, lots of sleep, feeling a bit sorry for yourself, but you will be fine.'

How had I not registered this at the time? I might have saved myself the trouble of spending New Year in Accident and Emergency getting my head stitched back together!

The tape reached the end.

'Stay in touch,' said Arthur.

I resolved to do just that and dashed off a letter to him. Little did I realize that this very letter would lead to 20 years of study with Arthur, during which I learned his reading techniques, bought countless books and packs of Tarot cards, and gave thousands of readings.

The cycle with Arthur reached its conclusion in March 2010 with his passing and me inheriting his materials, his cards and his centre – The Hermitage Development Centre. Quite a remarkable journey from our first encounter at a tiny psychic fayre all those years ago.

And by the way, I am writing this the morning after my blonde-haired friend's 40th birthday party!

◠

VIII

STRENGTH

with Geraldine Beskin

In a Tarot pack I have from the 1800s, the Strength card shows an elephant behind a woman. More often today, the illustration depicts a woman opening the jaws of a lion, king of the jungle.

The woman's tranquillity, concentration and deftness are to be applauded. She shows a maturity of attitude as she quietly dominates a beast that could turn on her at any moment. It won't, though. She has the inner strength to understand the mood of her potential foe. She has a great deal of experience physically and spiritually, and she does the only thing obvious to her – avert danger by dealing with it.

The greatest strength is in the willow reed that bends in the face of the wind. It is not about digging in and standing four-square against an onslaught. The Chinese sages in particular taught this. Usually a quiet word is more productive than a shouting match.

Strength shows us the potential we have to act well or badly. We interpret the meaning of the card and act on its advice. Sometimes this takes more of our strength than it does at other times!

Geraldine Beskin talks Tarot

My journey with Tarot began in the early 60s when my father owned The Atlantis Bookshop. I found all sorts of treasures in the shop, including aura goggles – those seem to have faded from fashion now – and an incomplete George Muchery pack that I was allowed to keep. I liked the bold colours, and the designs were very different to anything else I had seen.

All through the 70s and 80s we imported cards from the USA, and my mother and I enjoyed compiling albums of sample decks for people to choose cards from. I was terribly spoilt for choice; it was an exciting time, with the arrival of many varieties of decks along with new and radical interpretations of the cards. What an impact the Motherpeace pack had! It seems strange that until around 35 years ago, the Waite, Crowley and Marseilles versions of Tarot were all that were readily available in the UK.

My favourite decks were the Aquarian and the Thoth, and I learned Tarot with them. Now, the Aquarian cards seem elegant, cold and aloof, but how I loved them then. The Thoth is the Thoth is the Thoth – as a feast for the subconscious, nothing comes close.

My grandmother taught me to tell fortunes using playing cards, although I had to wait until I was nine years old! She showed me how the cards 'moved', 'warmed up', how colour was important. The high cards meant more than the low cards, and she taught me how to read a spread. It is lovely when 'the 'fluence is upon you', when a reading flows and you are really on song.

I use Tarot sparingly for 'proper' readings, as I know it will tell me True – even if I misinterpret what it says! Single-card readings are more frequent, but they can turn into three-card readings if I need to gain a little extra spin on a situation. Tarot is a super-sensual way of making sense of my universe. It is my friend and I delight in it.

⌢

IX

THE HERMIT
with Alfred Douglas

This card is numbered nine in the Major Arcana sequence. Nine stands at the peak of the single numbers and so it signifies the ending of the first stage of the quest. From here the path turns downwards.

The Hermit card depicts an old man, solitary like The Fool, and like The Fool he has embarked upon a journey. But unlike The Fool, he looks ahead at the ground before him with focused attention, taking care not to stray from his chosen path. With his stick he tests the way ahead carefully; he has not slung it casually over his shoulder as the carefree Fool has done. Life has taught The Hermit to be cautious and patient.

The Hermit carries a lantern to illuminate his path. Its golden flame burns with the light of the spirit, the alchemical quintessence released from the dark imprisonment of matter. But note that the light is still constrained within the confines of the lantern; partly to shield it from the unstable elements outside, and partly to protect those The Hermit encounters on the way from the blinding intensity of the divine spark he carries. As the lantern bearer, he displays to the world his grade as an initiate. In his steady gaze, he combines the guileless wonder of the innocent Fool with the patience and tolerance born of age and experience.

In his search for wisdom The Hermit has chosen a dark and solitary path. The scales of Justice – the previous card – have tipped from the outward-looking, solar half of life to the inner, lunar realm of dreams and the unconscious. Solitude activates the inner powers of the psyche that are no longer drowned out by the clamour of daily life, and that can guide us on the road to fulfilment.

In myths and fairy tales the Wise Old Man appears to guide the hero back to the true path from which he has strayed, and to offer trustworthy guidance. This is the role The Hermit plays when he is found in a Tarot spread.

Alfred Douglas talks Tarot

My interest in Tarot began back in the 50s when I was at school. My mother was given a copy of *Prediction* magazine each month by her best friend, and I started to read it because it was lying around the house. I became interested in all the topics I found there – astrology, palmistry, magic, paganism, the paranormal – and especially Tarot. Every month there was a two-page article on Tarot written by someone called Madeline Montalban. These articles touched on divination but were mainly devoted to examining the cards themselves and exploring the stories they might illustrate. Madeline was a gifted writer who had the ability to take a difficult and complex subject such as alchemy or Kabbalah, and use it to throw light on Tarot in a readable and entertaining way. I only realized how rare a gift this is many years later when I came to write about Tarot myself.

I met Madeline in person in London at the end of 1964, and was amazed when first I saw her sit at her big pre-war Imperial typewriter and write a Tarot article for *Prediction*. She produced a single draft only and never seemed to refer to any books. She was so immersed in the subject that she didn't need to.

Madeline's view of Tarot was that it embodied a rich seam of ancient wisdom that could be read by anyone who took the time to work out what the symbols meant. Easier said than done. But she must have started studying the occult at an early age. Like all adepts, there are strange gaps in her history, and she could be extremely elusive when asked about certain times in her life.

The earliest article by her that I have come across was a skilful piece about astrology published in *London Life* magazine in 1933, which proves she had established herself in London as a writer by the age of 23. Tarot articles followed.

Her articles in *Prediction* appeared from 1953 until her death in 1982, and were mostly illustrated by cards from The Thomson-Leng Tarot, which had been given away with women's magazines published by D.C. Thomson in 1936. Perhaps this was how she acquired her deck – but she never said. There was a lot that was never said, but she was an inspiring teacher who gave me a lifelong love of Tarot. And I am still trying to work out what the symbols mean.

⌁

Wheel of Fortune

X

WHEEL OF FORTUNE

with Rachel Pollack

Wheel of Fortune. I asked myself, what could I say about this? Then I remembered my poem 'Wheel of Fortune', which appears in my book *Fortune's Lover*. The poem ends with these lines:

We who read cards are Fortune's lovers,
intoxicated by other people's lives,
their memories like dreams we live in pictures,
their starts and detours and dead ends,
their round and round and round,
like a thick liqueur.
Their mistakes and triumphs spark in us
a shameless joy of images.
This is time illumined,
St Catherine's wheel of lives,
sweet Fortune's gift.

Rachel Pollack talks Tarot

I first heard of Tarot through T.S. Eliot's epic poem *The Wasteland* – which I read every April in honour of its opening line 'April is the cruellest month' – and the book that inspired it, *From Ritual To Romance*. Jessie L. Weston claims in the book that Tarot, and the Grail stories, descend from prehistoric Celtic mythology.

I don't think I ever thought I would see an actual pack, until one day in early spring 1970, when I was teaching college English and a fellow teacher offered to read my cards. The deck was the University Press edition of the Rider – the one with the ankh on the back, still my favourite. I knew I had to have it. To me the cards were frozen moments in unknown stories. The fact that with them we could discover and create the stories of people's lives made them all the more enticing.

Jump a few years. I had quit teaching to go and live in Amsterdam and write. A few of my stories sold but I needed more money to live, so I got a job cleaning a bar every afternoon. That is, until I was fired, four days before Christmas! I had limited Dutch and was an illegal alien, so, after considering my meagre options, I knocked on the very imposing carved door of the Kosmos Meditatie Centrum and said, 'I'd like to teach a class in Tarot.' My book *Seventy-Eight Degrees Of Wisdom* grew out of that class.

I did not expect to continue writing about Tarot, but one thing led to another. I had the idea for my book *Tarot Readings and Meditations*, its original title being *The Open Labyrinth*. Then I was asked to write the book for the Salvador Dali Tarot, and later the companion book to the brilliant Haindl Tarot, created by Hermann Haindl. I also wrote the accompanying book of The Vertigo Tarot for creators Neil Gaiman and Dave McKean.

I decided to create my own Tarot deck, The Shining Tribe. I intended to have a 'real' artist draw the illustrations, but when I read the cards for Niki de Saint Phalle in Paris, she told me she thought I should draw them myself.

In my most recent book, *The New Tarot Handbook*, I wrote this about the cards: 'I can say one thing with certainty – we will never come to the end of it.'

Tarot is as open as life and imagination, and Tarot people are among the finest in the world.

⟳

XI
JUSTICE
with Alison Cross

$\mathbf{S}$he is seated squarely on her stone bench and effortlessly holds aloft the symbols of her title – a sword and scales. Her name is Justice.

She sits between two great pillars with a veil stretched between them. Having the veil at her back assures her position is secure – no one can sneak up from behind to undermine her. Her pose is reminiscent of The High Priestess and much of the Priestess's silent watchful energy is also in the spirit of Justice.

Justice's sword is unsheathed, which immediately makes one feel a little frisson of excitement at the danger of it all. How will things work out? Will she find in my favour? But Justice holds her blade perfectly straight and balanced – as are her scales. Everything is weighed and balanced before she takes action.

I like her sense of fairness, of being prepared to wait until she's got all the facts at her fingertips. This encourages me to be patient and wait before taking action – again, an energy seeping through from The High Priestess.

She is, thanks to those scales, associated with the astrological sign of Libra and this air sign is perfect for her – logical, intelligent and communicative. See that blue square on her crown? That too assures me that she is airy in her approach to life.

Like The Magician, Justice is a lightning rod. Except she doesn't hold a double-headed wand like the figure of The Magician does; instead she holds up the cool blade of her sword as the conductor of the divine spark. Through that blade – and it can cut both ways – the transmission of universal justice enables her to balance her scales.

Of course, this doesn't mean that everything is guaranteed to go your way. But Justice does guarantee you will get what you deserve. Quite a different concept... perhaps a little scary too!

Alison Cross talks Tarot

Once upon a time – I bought myself a Marseilles Tarot deck and a copy of *The Tarot* by Alfred Douglas. They were, if memory serves me correctly, the only two Tarot items in the entire four-storey bookshop!

Of course, I could not read my new cards without the assistance of the LWB, but nevertheless I entertained myself with lengthy readings. One particular reading indicated that I would be unwell and looked after by my mother – a prediction I completely forgot about until I was on a trolley being whizzed through the corridors of my local hospital with a ruptured appendix. This was followed by a lengthy recuperation period at home with my mother! I know. Spooky! Somewhat freaked out, I put the books and cards away and simply got on with life. But I always felt a yearning towards Tarot.

In 2003, a TV programme that featured someone learning to read Tarot was a sufficient spur to make me knuckle down and study this amazing tool. I joined the Tarot Association of The British Isles and I never looked back!

I secured a place on TABI's free training course and soon after began writing reviews and articles for the members-only e-zine. From there I became the magazine's editor, a position held for over four years, and also contributed reviews and articles to other national magazines such as *Spirit & Destiny*. I went on to become Chairman of TABI, another position held for over four years. I stepped down in 2012 to focus my efforts on my own Tarot business, which includes my Tarot blog and website, and recently a weekly Tarot radio show on Radio Bute, Scotland. The creation of my own Oracle deck is under way.

⁓

XII

THE HANGED MAN

with Linda Hare

Suspended in the air I don't have a clue
But from this position I see more than you
Let go of all you think you are, become what you can be
And if you change your point of view
You will see as much as me

To me The Hanged Man will always be Odin, sacrificing what is for what could be. Sometimes we need to be suspended in space with the ground pulled from beneath our feet before we can allow ourselves to see things from a different perspective.

In most Tarot decks I have seen, The Hanged Man seems quite content with his position. His face is passive and he seems to have accepted that, for now, all he can do is hang around and wait. His world is indeed upside down, but he realizes that for the moment there is nothing he can do to change it.

This is the space of learning, it is time-out, and sometimes – although you would not have put yourself in this space – you can sense that he knows all will be well.

The Hanged Man knows who he is and knows that to others his point of view may sometimes seem out of place. He is an individual and enjoys his own quirky way of seeing things. He is not bothered by the opinions of others, who may see him as being stuck in a rut.

He knows the meaning of sacrifice, but in letting go of his ego he has found his true self and is content for now to see how things play out.

He must not, however, use his individuality as an excuse to behave in bizarre or inappropriate ways just for the sake of being seen as different. Being true to oneself does not have to be at the expense of alienating others.

This card requires a patient attitude and a faith in the Universe to put things back as they should be.

Linda Hare talks Tarot

I have always been a seeker of truth, and was blessed with a wonderful grandmother who encouraged me to ask questions. She was psychic and it was perfectly natural to me that she seemed to know things others did not. Growing up, I always asked the awkward questions and wanted to look at things from every angle before forming an opinion – and my opinion was often different from the norm.

At the age of 32, after studying many forms of religion and spiritual thought, I met a wonderful woman, Eileen Newport – a well-known medium in London leading up to and during the war years. She had retired to the seaside town where I lived and she formed a study circle. I was invited to join the circle and began a twelve-year study of all things esoteric.

Tarot was a big part of the study and I hated it! Brought up a Catholic, I believed Tarot was the Devil's picture book and I flatly refused to have anything to do with it. However, over time my natural curiosity and my need to see things from all angles won out, and I began to study it. First the imagery, then the history, and finally the meanings ascribed to the cards by various well-known writers.

Eventually the meanings made sense and I started to notice situations in my own life that mirrored the card meanings and spreads I was looking at. I started to do readings in earnest in 1983, and was surprised and delighted with the accuracy and insight the cards provided.

Needless to say, I sometimes see things from an upside-down point of view, so I was not surprised that The Hanged Man was chosen as my card. The Universe knows me well. Blessed be.

~

XIII

DEATH

with Lyn Howarth-Olds

There is no doubt that Death is a serious card, and of all the 78 cards in a Tarot pack, it is the one most likely to evoke uncertainty – perhaps even fear – in your querent.

Will I die? Will someone I love die? Even if they don't say, it is what the inexperienced enquirer is probably thinking. Address this card's presence in the reading before all others. Your sitter is unlikely to focus on anything else until you do! Some commentators are keen to rename the card in an attempt to soften its impact, but I don't feel the need. Its numbered position in the Major Arcana sequence reinforces to me that this is not the grand finale.

Things begin, things end – this cyclic pattern is a natural progression.

If you draw the Death card there is no escape. Something will change. And just as it is with physical death, the change may be sudden and out of the blue, or it may be long and drawn out. But as much as it can be hard to imagine at the time, more often than not what results is for the best.

Employment, friendships, relationships, living arrangements, perhaps a way of life – any of these areas in your life could be in for a shake-up when the Death card reveals itself. Accompanying cards in the spread will help you determine where and how you can expect this change to manifest.

If you have been struggling with something, the struggle is about to end. If you are stuck in a rut, a new chapter is about to unfold. Will you speed the process along with acceptance, or fight it all the way, resisting the change it brings?

At its extreme, a crippling fear of change or death itself may be present. A paralysis sets in, preventing any forward movement and the ability to live life to the full. This road must be negotiated carefully.

With every ending there is a new beginning, and while Death taketh away, by default it also restores and renews. So, in closing, I will borrow the title of the Blue Oyster Cult song and say, 'Don't fear the Reaper'!

Lyn Howarth-Olds talks Tarot

When Tarot and I first met, it was the 70s and I was 13 years old. I had a copy of Fred Gettings' *The Book of Tarot* from the school library, and a newly acquired – somewhat garishly coloured – Waite Tarot Card deck I had purchased from a local book and stationery store.

Sadly our relationship was short-lived. The Death card made an appearance in my very first reading and it certainly didn't help that the fold-out pamphlet that came with the cards – in its explanation for the Death card – read: 'It can also signify phisical [sic] death... from the divinatory viewpoint it can indicate a necessary end, sadness, pain, grief, disorder, corruption...'

I suspect the situation was made even worse given the card fell in a position in the spread, which, according to the fold-out pamphlet, represented: 'negative forces... predicts unfavourable things, what should be avoided. Thus, it stands for difficulties, dangers and enemies that will be encountered.'

I don't recall if I went on to read Mr Gettings' version of the card in order to get a second opinion. If I had, I'm guessing at the time, I probably would have only focused on the paragraph that included: 'Death indicates transformation, unavoidable death...'

Given my tender years, I can probably be forgiven for packing up the cards there and then. I remember being too frightened to throw them away and they were banished to the very back corner of a drawer under my bed. Having them buried under layers of unused clothing offered me some comfort.

In my late 20s my interest in Tarot rekindled and I have since taken classes, read cards, taught classes, organized Tarot events and conferences, and taken part in and hosted a number of Tarot art projects.

I came across my original Tarot deck some 25 years after it had been unfairly neglected and unjustly condemned. Thankfully it had survived a number of moves and had been kept – along with a few other precious items – in a box marked 'don't throw out'. I have never been able to trace the deck's publishing origins; neither the box nor the pamphlet offer any clues as to where it might have been printed.

⌐

XIV

TEMPERANCE

with Juliet Sharman Burke

In our age of excess, Temperance can act as a moderating influence. We are beset by extremes – too hot, too cold; too wet, too dry; too rich, too poor; too fat, too thin – and we need something temperate and fair to balance these intense opposites.

The angel of Temperance stands with one foot in the water and the other on dry land, carefully pouring liquid from one cup to the other – suggesting mixing, combining and sharing in equal measure. She is meticulous in her task, unlike The Star maiden, who pours her water freely and with an air of joyful abandon. Temperance is thoughtful, careful and considerate, and as this is a card that can represent feelings and relationships, the angel illustrates a prudent and watchful approach to her task of mixing and pouring the liquid without spilling a drop. We need a degree of caution in our approach to personal as well as collective issues, as we combine thoughts and feelings, sensation and intuition, and try to apply them fairly and equably to individual and global situations.

The Rider Waite Deck shows irises growing in the pool beside Temperance, which call to mind Iris, the goddess of the rainbow

– a luminous symbol of promise and renewal. The goddess in myth acts as a messenger who can move easily from the realms of the gods to the underworld, suggesting the easy movement between the conscious and unconscious mind. The path in the distance winding between the mountains reflects the middle way.

I really like this gentle card with its message of inclusiveness and sense of cooperation and compromise.

Juliet Sharman Burke talks Tarot

I came to Tarot quite by chance about 40 years ago. In an obscure bookshop, my friend and I came across a book by Stuart Kaplan, which suggested that one could read one's future in the cards. Being young and curious, we bought the book and accompanying deck and proceeded to try them out. It was not as easy as it looked and my friend soon lost interest, but I persevered, fascinated by the mysterious images.

As I practised reading for friends, I discovered the cards revealed things – that despite knowing the people well – I was completely unaware of.

There were several surprising instances when the cards hinted at relationship and personal difficulties with people who I believed were in a good place. By reading the meaning of the cards, rather than what I understood to be true, the cards turned out to be uncannily accurate.

Card choices were limited in those days. I started with a Marseilles deck, but when I came across Waite's I was really hooked. Easy-to-read books were also hard to find. After reading *The Devil's Picturebook* by Paul Huson, I started to see the connections with myth and astrology, and went on to study both with Liz Greene.

I came to realize that many people who sought readings had complex psychological problems, so I started training as a psychotherapist. This helped enormously with my understanding of people's emotional issues.

I ran workshops for beginners and a magazine article came out about them. It drew a huge response from people all over the country, requesting I create a correspondence course. My first book came out of that course. Later, Liz Greene and I worked on the idea of combining Tarot, myth and psychology in The Mythic Tarot.

~

XV

The Devil

XV

THE DEVIL

with Kim Arnold and Aleister Crowley

The Devil brings to the forefront our fears, negativity, pessimism and attachments, and signifies overindulgence and addictions.

When The Devil appears, we must decide if we have allowed ourselves to be restrained by the chains that bind and, if so, work out how we can release them. I try and help my clients look for ways to free themselves, and to understand that most negative situations are of our own making, or at least within our control to change for the better.

I always know that when this card shows in a reading, the querent has a life-changing choice or opportunity ahead – if they are prepared to be brave enough to make the necessary changes.

Whenever I see The Devil in my own reading, I know I have allowed myself to be overburdened and I need to look at how I can restore the balance of work and play.

Aleister Crowley by Kim Arnold

Aleister Crowley was born Edward Alexander Crowley in 1875. He was convinced he was the reincarnation of the magician Eliphas Levi, who had died the year Crowley was born.

Crowley was an occultist, mystic and ceremonial magician, and was responsible for creating the religious philosophy of Thelema. He was the son of wealthy upper-class parents and a highly intelligent man, born with many privileges. He inherited a vast amount of money from his father – who died when Crowley was 11 – and later he used this wealth to indulge in everything to the extreme; including drugs, prostitutes and decadent living.

Crowley came to my mind many years ago on a visit to Loch Ness in Scotland. Our tour guide pointed out Boleskine House, where Crowley lived from the age of 25. I was in awe at the isolation of this large, lonely-looking house nestling in the middle of nowhere. The stillness of the beautiful scenery surrounding the property was inspirational. But the rest of the tour party could only gasp in horror when the guide described Crowley as 'the most evil man on earth'.

It is said that strange things went on behind closed doors at the house, including Crowley allegedly summoning up demons. Who knows what truly went on, but since Crowley's death in 1947, the house has been plagued with violent deaths and poltergeist activity, and is said to be a house of 'bad vibes'.

Crowley was sometimes known as 'The Great Beast 666', so it is fitting to have him as our representative for The Devil card.

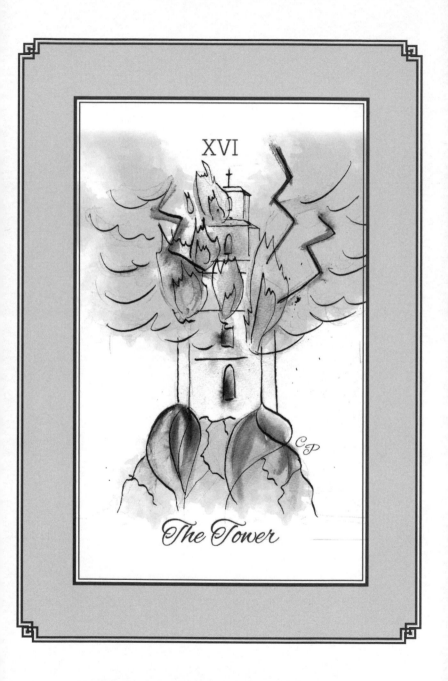

XVI

THE TOWER

with Carrie Paris

'In chaos, there is fertility.'
ANAÏS NIN

The thunderous crack that follows the lightning in this card makes a loud, radical cry for change. It transmits its message through a variety of earth-shaking notes and, like the music from the Gods, some notes will soothe the soul while others will shatter everything you know. Yet in the end, all invite us to pay close attention and listen more intently to the fertile and timeless message that resides within.

What are you choosing to listen to, and more importantly, what are you choosing to hear? The Tower's song is one that wakes us from a routine of listening to excuses and justifications. It shakes our very foundation until we become fully conscious of the messages and beliefs we give a strong ear to. It reminds us to get back in rhythm with what really matters, or else – like the couple fleeing in this card, we will be evicted from our comfort zones until we get it right.

What is taking precedence in your life: your happiness or keeping up appearances? By choosing the latter, you are inviting a cataclysmic event to put you back in touch with what has meaning.

If a crisis – no matter how large or small – is disrupting your foundation due to a misalignment with your truth, now is the time to ask, how long am I willing to keep the structure of false beliefs standing and at what cost?

Carrie Paris talks Tarot

'Wisdom cannot be stolen – it can only be shared.'
JEFFERSON SMITH, STRANGE PLACES

As a teen I spent a number of summer days hanging out in a California head-shop. It was a small boutique, filled with a large number of exotic items. What captured my attention most was a display of Tarot decks situated on a rich burgundy tablecloth, complete with crystal balls, candles and incense. I recall touching and smelling the unopened decks at every available opportunity. They were mysterious and alluring and I just had to know what was inside. One day, while the store owner had his back turned, the impulse to steal a deck overrode my fear of getting caught. Down the back of my pants went a Rider Waite, followed by a quick exit and dash home. It didn't take long for my mother to figure out my wrongdoing, so back to the shop she and my father took me to confess my crime.

Long story short, the store-owner delivered my fateful sentence – for the remaining summer I was to help clean his shop at closing. After the floor had been vacuumed and the rubbish put to bin, he would take a few minutes to teach me something new about the cards. I recall his deck being different to my newly 'acquired' Rider Waite and now know it to be a Marseilles, though at the time I didn't have a clue.

I eventually took his lessons to heart and branched out on my own, seeking out teachers wherever I lived. Each new teacher added greatly to my Tarot experience, though I still find myself returning to the very basic teachings given to me during that destined summer in California.

XVII

THE STAR

with Corrine Kenner

Physicists often point out that we are literally made of stardust. Our bodies are composed of atoms from the Big Bang, and elements that were forged in the fiery cores of ancient stars. The very essence of our being was flung through heaven, ages before the earth was formed.

What most people don't realize is that we owe much of our humanity to the stars, too. The stars helped shape our culture and civilization, as well as our consciousness and psyche. If we didn't have the stars, we wouldn't be the people we've become.

The stars, in short, gave us both our substance and our stories.

For thousands of years, people have gathered around campfires, gazed at the night sky, and spun stories on strands of starlight. In fact, every constellation can be linked to a timeless tale of a shared belief in a universe that's much bigger than ourselves.

The ancient Greeks and Romans believed that the stars were the physical manifestations of the gods. In fact, they thought that the planets – the 'wandering stars' – were the gods themselves, crossing the heavens against the backdrop of the zodiac.

Other cultures told similar stories, often linked to the timeless qualities of hope, faith and the endurance of the human spirit. Some people believed that stars were heroes who deserved places of honour in the heavens, or the souls of those who had crossed over into the great beyond.

Those myths and legends were the foundation of a primal psychology, and an understanding of the human condition that has been passed down, generation after generation.

The night sky has also shaped our sense of destiny. The stars guided the development of civilization by steering travellers across land and sea, in search of trade, conquest and exploration. The study of the stars gave us astrology – the precursor of modern maths and science. Today, the stars still inspire us to travel to new frontiers of technology and communication.

It's human nature to look for patterns in the stars – and in the cards. Tarot offers us a starting point for the stories of our lives, told by firelight and candlelight, across the Tarot reader's table. And no card summarizes our universal story better than The Star card – a clear and vivid reminder of the human experience, past, present and future.

Corrine Kenner talks Tarot

I was a writer before I was a Tarot reader. I worked my way through college as a newspaper reporter, and then I moved into a career as an editor and author.

In fact, it was writing that led me to the cards. In 1996, I went to work for Llewellyn Publishing – one of the world's largest distributors of Tarot decks and books – and I fell in love with the symbols and the stories of the cards.

The imagery wasn't entirely new to me. As a child of the 70s, I had grown up with astrology – even if it was only the pop-culture version of the art. In college, during the 80s, I majored in philosophy, and I spent most of my time immersed in the myths, legends and literature of ancient Greece. Even so, I had never seen those stories laid out as clearly – or as artistically – as I found them in Tarot.

The structure of the deck itself was a revelation. There's a cosmology in the cards, built into the design of the Major and Minor Arcana – which means that every deck comes complete with ready-made categories for every possible human experience. Until I started studying Tarot, I had only seen philosophers describe that cosmology in theoretical terms.

The cards give us a framework for understanding our lives, and a timeline for measuring our growth. The cards make it possible to visualize the past, present, and future – both in theory, and in practice. The cards help us celebrate our successes and understand our disappointments, so we can manage both. The cards help us put our hopes and fears into words – and in the process, Tarot helps us understand ourselves and our place in the world.

Most importantly, Tarot lets us share our stories with others. We all share the same Fool's Journey – but when we shuffle the cards, we all see our own stories come to life.

Tarot is the simplest, most effective way I've ever found to tell a story. The cards have inspired me to write – and keep writing – in hopes of helping other people tell their stories, too.

⌐∽

XVIII

THE MOON

with Cilla Conway

This is a challenging card that refers to the deep unconscious, to the borderland between what we call reality and what we see as fantasy and illusion. A few – like the ancient shamans – can walk over that border and come back. But others may get lost in the dream world and never return.

The Moon brings with it threat and promise, terror and ecstasy, grandiosity and paranoia. When The Moon appears you may feel at the mercy of another's deception, or perhaps even your own. You may experience delusions or a psychic invasion. However, if you are brave enough, you can work with the energy of The Moon to reflect your own inner light. By using creative work – writing, art, dance or voice – you can express the shadow energies of the collective unconscious, and the work produced will shimmer with archetypal forces.

The ancient priestesses acknowledged The Moon as a goddess. Today, if you allow, you can still feel her power.

Cilla Conway talks Tarot

A TV programme introduced me to Tarot in 1972, but at the time there were so few decks on the market that I started painting my own – a very poor medieval-inspired set that I eventually sold outright to Stuart Kaplan of US Games. My real journey began one evening when I was idly doodling and found I'd drawn The Fool. But he was a very different Fool from any I'd seen previously. His eyes, compelling and slightly insane, summoned me into his world. I followed – how could I not? He was calling me to my soul's work! The next evening I designed The Magician, then Justice, The Moon and Strength.

Alfred Douglas's book *The Tarot* introduced me to Jung and the mystery religions, and I discovered the Waite and Crowley Tarot decks.

Some cards in my deck were easy to create. Some, like The Devil, The Empress and The World, were harder. I had no intention of designing the Minors, but in 1978 they started appearing – so easily! The deck was finished in 1981, and in 2004 was published as The Intuitive Tarot.

I now read professionally; I'm designing an exciting new deck, and still following The Fool.

～

The Sun

XIX

THE SUN

with Sasha Fenton

Here is a précis of The Sun from my first book, written back in 1984: This lovely card signifies joy and happiness, and this may touch any area of your life. If there has been a health problem or some other worry, there could hardly be a nicer card to find. Efforts will be rewarded, trials overcome and there will be good friends, comfort and happiness. A marriage will be happy and filled with unselfish love and fun. Enterprises will go well, especially exams or business matters. I often see this card appear before the birth of a child, and this is a good omen if there are doubts about fertility. There may be a connection to grandchildren, neighbourhood children or work that involves children. Travel can be indicated, especially holidays in the sun. Sometimes the summer months are important for success and happiness.

If you use reversed cards, there is potential for happiness, but the picture is clouded. Success and achievement will take time, as will complete satisfaction from one's endeavours. There may be sadness concerning a child or a marriage.

Sasha Fenton talks Tarot

In 1975, my mother – knowing my interest in astrology – bought me a Tarot kit from the stationery store she was working in. The kit contained the IJJ Swiss Tarot deck, a book, and a paper template featuring a Celtic Cross design.

Keen to give Tarot reading a go, I took the kit to work. A friend and I had the contents of the box spread all over my desk – we had not counted on the boss walking in! My boss was a very important man, who had organized all the oil installations in Saudi Arabia, and given Tarot was considered occult in those days we couldn't imagine what he might have been thinking. He collected up the contents of the kit and walked out, telling us to come to his office the next day. We were too nervous to argue, or complain about the loss of my kit.

Naturally, we kept our appointment and to our utter astonishment, we found him at his desk with the paper spread out before him and cards in hand.

He proceeded to give first Kay, and then me, the most stunningly accurate readings we've ever experienced!

Oh, and yes, he did return my kit afterwards.

~

XX

JUDGEMENT

with Mark McElroy

The clouds part and Gabriel, the angel who announces births, appears in the sky. He lifts his trumpet. His cheeks puff out. The force of that thunderous note unfurls a flag emblazoned with a quadrate cross, a reminder that all of time – the four seasons, and all of space – the four directions, hinge on this moment.

The church of my childhood was obsessed with Judgement Day. We wanted reunions with lost loved ones. We wanted new bodies, immune to the corruptions of sickness and age. We longed to see the parted clouds, the fiery angel, the victorious Christ.

And, in some dark corner of our hearts, we also wanted to say, 'We told you so'. You sinners chose a life of dancing, drinking, and lazy Sundays in bed, while we saints chose to sit soberly in hard wooden pews. Judgement Day would show, once and for all, who had made the best choices.

As an adult, I no longer expect a literal Judgement Day. But I do include in my patchwork faith a belief in the metaphorical truth of Judgement. There's value in reflecting on progress, in weighing options, in taking stock. Have today's choices moved me closer to my goals? Have today's actions brought me closer to the life I want to live?

This approach to Judgement doesn't court the approval of an external god, nor does it offer comforting delusions of self-righteousness. Instead, it requires us to do the difficult work of staying awake in a sleeping world. We have to know where we are. We have to know where we want to go. And we have to acknowledge that every choice we make, every minute of every day, either supports or hinders our progress towards our goals.

For me, the Judgement trump is a reminder that every moment is an opportunity to align my choices with my goals. Will I eat leafy greens or a chocolate cake? Will I go running, or will I watch TV? Will I work on that novel, or piddle away the hours online?

Or, to borrow the perspective of the Judgement card itself: will I stay nestled in my box, lulled to sleep beneath the turf of an unexamined life – or will I rise, naked and vulnerable, and become something new?

Anyone can wait around for an angel. It's much harder – and far more rewarding – to plot our own course, gauge our own progress, and put our God-given Judgement to good use.

Mark McElroy talks Tarot

I bought my first Tarot deck when I was nine years old. It came from Spencer Gifts, the same store in our local mall that sold fake vomit, lava lamps, blacklight posters and hookahs.

For many months afterwards, I terrorized the other neighbourhood nine-year-olds with dire and dramatic predictions.

My favourite trick? Stacking the deck so that Pamela Colman Smith's wonderful Death card popped up, again and again, in a spread position I called, 'What Absolutely Must Happen to You Tomorrow'.

I forgot about Tarot until 1999, when I was smack in the middle of my atheist phase. I got involved with divination to debunk it – and discovered, to my surprise, there was real value in spending quiet moments exploring options and generating ideas with the I Ching or *Book of Changes*.

When friends had trouble connecting with the I Ching's obscure language and pages of text, I went looking for a more visual oracle and came back to Tarot. Curious about the stories behind the cards, I started reading A.E. Waite's *Pictorial Key to the Tarot*.

After slogging my way through that exquisite swamp of a text, I went looking for more accessible works, and found great books by Papus, Wirth, Gareth Knight, Paul Foster Case, Aleister Crowley, Alexander Jodoworsky, Mary K. Greer, (the under-appreciated) Joan Bunning, Julia Turk, Jana Riley, Hajo Banzhaf and Sandra Thomson.

Online, I stumbled on the warm and welcoming community that was the original Comparative Tarot. There, two wonderful things happened: I expanded my appreciation for the variety of Tarot decks out there, and I met the delightful Barbara Moore, who became both my editor and my friend.

In the years after that, I had the pleasure of writing five Tarot books and designing seven Tarot decks of my own. I met amazing people along the way: Tarot readers, other authors, talented writers, publishers – at Llewellyn and Lo Scarabeo, and event organizers such as Wald and Ruth Ann Amberstone of the Readers' Studio in New York, and Kim Arnold and her intrepid husband, Martin.

At some point though, Tarot became more work than play. I went back to a corporate job and, for the first time in ages, my cards gathered dust.

After a long break, I'm rediscovering Tarot with fresh eyes. I'm not sure where this new Tarot journey will take me. For now, I'm just happy: happy to hear from old friends, happy to be reading the cards again, and happy to feel a renewed connection with the wisdom of the Tarot deck.

⌒

XXI

The World

XXI

THE WORLD

with Riccardo Minetti

I expect most people will be familiar with the basic meanings of The World. It is usually seen as a card of completion, with the assumption that we journey in a line from one place – The Magician or The Fool – to another, The World. From small to large, from beginning to end. I wonder if this is actually true.

Perhaps it would be better to see the journey as a circle, and not as a line. This way The World can also be seen as the first step of a journey back; from an ending to a new beginning, from large to small. And rather than being a destination, The World can become the journey itself.

Actually I think that if you want to understand The World, it is important to look past its basic meaning of expansion.

I will borrow from psychology, specifically Urie Bronfenbrenner and his ecological systems theory. Bronfenbrenner described the development of individual personality as the continual interaction of the self with the world. Like concentric spheres, we have our inner being located at the centre.

The world is first the person we are, then family, then friends, then the working environment. We expand, and as we grow, the world becomes our town, our country, our ethnicity, and finally the human race and all living things.

If you look at The World in this way, you will see it as the Arcanum of interconnection and relationship. It is a symbol of our place within the world, and of the place the world has within self.

I don't believe it is wise to try to further restrict the definition of The World. Each time we look at the card we are looking through a window. Even with the clearest glass and the widest angle, there will always be more.

In the end, we spend our life not trying to understand The World, but living within it, experiencing a little more of it with every breath we take.

Riccardo Minetti talks Tarot

I started working with Tarot in high school to try to impress a girl. I guess it was not meant to be. She was too fond of the Marseilles, while I couldn't seem to limit myself to one single deck.

My real Tarot journey started when I began working at Lo Scarabeo. In my time there I have had the privilege of meeting and listening to some of the greatest Tarot minds of our day, and have had the opportunity to see many decks being created from start to finish. As a result I learn new things about Tarot daily and I love it!

I am not esoteric. I'm not even an experienced reader. But I like to think that me and Tarot, well, we kind of know each other – we are buddies who like to hang out.

⌒

XXII

THE PATH

with Kim Arnold

*'March on. Do not tarry. To go forward is to move
toward perfection. March on, and fear not the
thorns, or the sharp stones on life's path.'*
KHALIL GIBRAN

In the process of creating this deck, The Path card was channelled to me. My initial thought was that we could not have 23 Major Arcana cards, but the vision of the man standing at the beginning of the crossroads was so powerful, it just had to be included. I queried as to why this card should be number 22, then delving into my limited knowledge of numerology, I realized it was a perfect match. Twenty-two is a powerful number, the positive aspect of which can turn dreams into reality. Adversely, the negative aspect is that it can create pressure and stress.

If you look at the card you will see two paths – one of turmoil and one of positive energy. The message of The Path is not to rush to make major decisions. Weigh up the pros and cons before stepping forward and most importantly, be guided by the card which follows The Path; it will help you make the right choice. However, remember that whatever you do in the moment, whether it is ultimately right or wrong, there was a reason for your decision; sometimes the darker path is the one we must take to learn and grow.

The Path card represents the choices we have to make and that each decision has a consequence. When we learn to trust our intuition we are more likely to make the right choice.

～

PART TWO

MORE
TAROT
MASTERS

INTRODUCTION

Everyone featured in this book has made an impact in the Tarot world. This section of the book features inspiring teachers and authors, along with artists and readers, many of whom travel the world to spread their knowledge of the Tarot. Each was asked to share their story of how their journey with the Tarot began, specifically what made them pick up a deck of Tarot for the first time, where it all began and the card that they love or loathe the most. All is revealed in the pages that follow...

CIRO MARCHETTI

talks Tarot...

I cannot recall a specific beginning to my Tarot journey because I was always casually aware of Tarot's existence, along with the usual layman's assumption that the cards were in some manner used for 'fortune telling'. But the first time I actually saw Tarot decks and examined them in a more direct way was at a book fair in Miami. I bought two, both variations of Marseilles.

The images of the Majors intrigued me; the Minor Arcana also piqued my curiosity because they seemed familiar. As a child my mother had taught me to play an Italian game of cards called 'scopa' or 'sweep or broom', where one sweeps the table clean of cards by winning tricks. Of the four suits coins were the most powerful, serving as trumps before the Major Arcana trumps were incorporated. The Seven of Coins was the most powerful card of all. It is part of Italian culture in fact: the Settebello, or 'beautiful seven', was the name given to a luxury express train – one of the few trains of the Italian railway system that arrived on time! I'm sure that variations of scopa date back many centuries and have some connection to the earlier use of Tarocchi decks for game playing.

Having said all that, I have to admit that my initial interest in Tarot was purely aesthetic. I loved the images without having a clue about the symbolism behind them. I mounted the cards in a frame and hung them on a wall rather than attempting to read with them, shameful on my part no doubt, but that is where they remained – unmoved for about 10 years – until Llewellyn approached me with the suggestion of producing a deck of my own.

My initial reaction was that I didn't know enough about Tarot to embark on such a project, and I informed Llewellyn accordingly. Nevertheless, they felt that what they had seen in my other work suggested there was something there – some potential that might lend itself to a Tarot deck. With that encouragement I bit the bullet. After all, it seemed like a really interesting challenge.

The Gilded Tarot did turn out to be a fascinating project, which I thoroughly enjoyed working on and learning from. But a greater inspiration came after the fact, and was really a consequence of the feedback on that first deck rather than the actual process of producing it. I began to realize and appreciate the uniqueness of Tarot. I found that compared to other creative fields – fine art, music, literature and movies – the collective body of work that a Tarot deck represents far surpasses all others in terms of how its users would respond and interact. The symbiotic relationship created between a reader and this 'tool' compelled me to do better on each subsequent deck I created. On each occasion, while not straying too far from the norm, I tried to communicate the concept of each card in a more compelling way, while adding a stamp of personal style.

The next eight years were occupied on an almost full-time basis with the production of several other decks: The Tarot of Dreams, The Legacy of the Divine Tarot, The Oracle of Dreams, a complete reworking of my original deck into its richer Gilded Royale version, and finally the Gilded Reverie Lenormand.

...and The Fool

The Fool has to be my favourite card of the Major Arcana. How can it not be? It's me! But then of course, it's everybody. The start of The Fool's journey is applicable to so many aspects of our lives. It can serve as an analogy for our whole lives or for a brief experience within it. How can we not relate to the many leaps of faith as we step off our various cliffs? Sometimes we leap with courage, sometimes with fear. Sometimes we are well prepared, sometimes it's a spontaneous impulse. But we never know for sure what may be involved and what the outcome will be.

The Fool's innocence is the very quality that gives all our decisions a twist. Our courage may be false because we are unaware of the dangers ahead. Is that what the little white dog snapping at our feet is trying to warn us about? When there is fear it may be for a reason or it may be completely unwarranted – imaginings of dangers that do not exist.

Our canine companion may in fact be encouraging us to move on. Either way, we are constantly taking symbolic first steps. The people we meet, and the circumstances we face in our careers and relationships, are all lessons to be learned as we progress towards our own World card.

ADELE NOZEDAR

talks Tarot...

My gran gave me a Marseilles deck when I was about eight. A weird present to give to a child, but then she was like that. I suspect it might have been an unwanted present she had received... she was like that, too!

I thought the deck was fascinating. I loved the pictures, although I didn't really understand what they were. I just played with them. It was a good way to learn Tarot, as I would find out later.

When I was 11, the James Bond movie *Live and Let Die* was released. After seeing it, I became rather enamoured by Fergus Hall's Tarot of the Witches, and I saved up my pocket money and bought my own deck. The idea that cards should be gifted rather than bought for oneself is cute, but I don't follow it! This deck remains one of my favourites.

Later, I found a very old deck at a car-boot sale, well-used and greasy. The pips were marked as 'normal' playing cards, and the relationship between a Tarot deck and the packs of cards we used for playing gin rummy suddenly became clear.

In 2003, under odd circumstances, I met up with a distant relative, Beryl Nozedar, in Los Angeles. Beryl is a psychic who travels the world giving Tarot readings and she was working at a place called The Psychic Eye. I don't have many relatives and she became a good friend. She told me that the best way to learn about Tarot was to buy a book about it, but never read it!

And then things got even odder... but that's a different story.

...and The Fool

I love the idea that the characters of Tarot can be any of us at any time, reflecting a complex state of emotions, situations, problems and victories. Although it is hard to choose, I love The Fool more than any other card. For me, he encapsulates the germ of an idea and the birth of possibilities; he is about optimism and ideas. He represents the ignorance of youth, but nevertheless manages to accomplish great things.

Not every genius idea works, but there's nothing worse than someone picking holes in one before you've started. The Fool is a child setting out for university, someone starting a business, someone sitting under a tree in the sun watching the flowers grow. Someone falling in love, possibly with the wrong person... but falling in love nevertheless.

I love that The Fool later becomes wise. But I never want him to lose that 'let's just do it' exuberance which, for me, is an essential part of his nature.

I love, too, that The Fool's number is that big fat zero. It can mean nothing, but when added to another number it increases it tenfold. It's also symbolic of the universe, the never-ending circle... not so foolish after all.

Maybe the invigorating spark of life, naiveté and blind faith belonging to The Fool is just what's needed to leaven any inspiration and transform an idea into reality.

⌒

NAOMI OZANIEC

talks Tarot...

It is not difficult for me to choose my most beloved Tarot image, nor is it hard to remember when and where I encountered it – even though it was many years ago. In 1977 to be more precise. In those days Tarot still carried a certain mystique, hovering somewhere between the dangerous and the bizarre. In today's easy Tarot-times, it is difficult to convey this atmosphere. At 26, I had never even seen a Tarot card, and I knew not a single thing about the subject.

At the time, I was part of an Aquarian discussion group. The New Age had not yet taken over the High Street, and esoteric subjects were still in the shadows. Even joining such a group called for a little personal courage and an independence of spirit. It was a clarion call for the spiritually disenfranchised, the rebellious, perhaps even the mildly eccentric.

I can still remember a certain frisson of excitement as the room darkened and new and fascinating images were lit up on the screen. Straight away, I fell in love with the images from the Thoth Tarot. This was the first Tarot deck I became familiar with. The image of The Fool still appears as large in my mind as it did in that room, now exaggerated in proportion and power.

It was here I encountered the name of Isis for the first time. As we studied Trump II, The High Priestess – She of the Silver Star – Isis came into my life. In that single moment my life changed. As I heard Her name spoken outside the confines of myth, something deep within me awoke. I felt a resonance that I did not understand. Though I did not know it then, She had found me and I had found Her.

Her image opened a door almost like the fictional wormhole between worlds. Though I did not know it, Isis was to take my hand and lead me on a personal journey that would last 45 years.

My journey is not complete, and it all began in that simple moment when I gazed upon Her image.

...and The High Priestess

I am the High Priestess. Welcome to the temple within. This place is open to all who seek the inner life of the soul with true intent. I hold the book of life in my lap. Is it your wish to know what is written here in the scroll of law? What will you do with such knowledge? Do not mistake knowledge for gnosis. Only gnosis can nourish the soul. If you seek me, I will bring you to wisdom. I dwell within the Temple of the Mysteries of Being and Becoming. I sit between the pillars of life, the eternal polarity that emerges from the one. My number is two, which is the dynamic polarity of manifestation. See the veil at my back that is decorated with pomegranates, the many-seeded fruit of the Goddess. Glimpse beyond the veil. See the vast ocean. It is whole of itself, virgin perfection. It is the universal energy beneath and within all life. It is the great ocean, eternal life itself. I serve the Ancient Wisdom. I uphold the light of the Mysteries. This is my domain – the holy temple of being and becoming – and I am the servant upon the throne. I am the eternal servant of the Great Goddess whose names are without number. Where She is I am to be found, and She is to be found at all times and in all places, whether secretly or openly. This is her temple and I am her servant. My inner mind has been opened and awakened to the invisible realms. My mind has been changed through long apprenticeship. I know the secrets of the ways of Being and Becoming. The Moon is attributed to my realm. It is the inner light. See the moon at my feet. Moon magic is mine, as it is the magic of all women who remember the Divine by Her own name. See that my robe resembles the waters. Moon and water hold the ebb and flow of life between them. I have access to the living waters within. I know the ways of the psyche and how it may be nourished. I am your capacity for wisdom and deep understanding. I bring compassion and gnosis. I am your realization of the mystery of life. If you see me in a spread, I affirm your power to be intuitive and find your own wisdom. I am the High Priestess in you.

~

LISA TENZIN-DOLMA

talks Tarot...

I was 26 years old when I first met Tarot. I'd been studying astrology, numerology and the I Ching for a while, and a friend showed me his Rider Waite Tarot deck. I was entranced by the symbolism in the images and the way the cards 'spoke' to me.

I acquired my own deck and decided to meditate on each card before reading any interpretations. For several weeks the images infused my dreams as each card gifted me with its story.

I have always seen Tarot as a journey, with each image embodying an aspect of self and a step along the path of life. It is this that inspires me to work closely with the cards, and to use them to help others find their path when they feel they have lost their way.

I admire the way that every deck is beautiful and unique; a product of the imagination of its illustrator.

Creating a Tarot deck is a journey in itself, a quest that ploughs the deepest furrows in the artist's psyche. I discovered this for myself when I created The Glastonbury Tarot.

We instinctively respond powerfully to images, colours, shapes and symbols: When these come together in a deck, Tarot becomes an extraordinary portal for self-understanding.

...and The Empress

It's hard to choose just one card, because my favourite may change from day to day or moment to moment! But one I particularly love is The Empress, because it so beautifully resonates with my passion for all forms of creativity.

Fecundity of the mind filters through to deep experience and expression of the emotions, manifesting into the physical in a way that can enrich both the creator and the witness.

Here's what I wrote about The Empress for my book *The Glastonbury Tarot*:

'The Empress card symbolizes the energy of a full-blooded woman, a lover and mother figure. Whereas The High Priestess connects us with the intuitive, subtle aspects of femininity that can seem almost intangible – and with the expression of the mind into form – The Empress is the power of woman that is firmly earthed and anchored, that is passionately emotional, and has strong needs and desires that can override reason.

'The marriage of Card I, the will, and Card II, the inner power, creates Card III. A state of harmony and synthesis, a new creative and procreative energy. The Empress can be seen as the union of The Magician and The High Priestess, the child that is brought into being. In a reading, this can signify a physical child, or the birth of an idea or vision that can be nurtured.

'The Empress symbolizes a time of growth, a harmonizing process, and the birth of fresh and exciting energy in your life. It is the feeling of passion; of being prepared to

give all that you have to whatever you are involved in.
You are likely to be feeling an urge to indulge yourself,
and to create pleasure for those around you.'

This card teaches you how to connect with your emotions and allow yourself to truly feel them and express them. It also signifies an upsurge of creativity that could prove to be beneficial in both the material and emotional areas of your life.

⌒

ADAM FRONTERAS

talks Tarot...

⁓ ᙨᙩᙲᙩᙨ ⁓

I had my first psychic experiences seeing the spirits of children who had passed away when I was young and in hospital. As a child I suffered terribly with asthma and was regularly in hospital care – often for long periods of time – and, at one point, I was even confined to an oxygen tent.

During one stay at Great Ormond Street in the early 70s, my parents brought me in a boxed Tarot set to help me pass the time. They had spotted the set in a shop window on their way to visit. There were not many shops selling Tarot cards at that time – let alone displaying them in their front windows – and so I suspect, given the location of the hospital, the shop was probably Atlantis. The deck in the set was the IJJ Swiss and it came with a paperback book by Stuart Kaplan.

I entertained the hospital staff with my readings. If there is one thing that will get nurses sitting on your bed, it is reading them their future in the cards! A Spanish cleaner I had read for told my mother, 'Your boy has the gift of the eye.' These words were a little disconcerting for Mum with her Catholic upbringing!

A year or two after receiving my first deck of cards, the James Bond film *Live and Let Die* came out, and I was gifted a set of the Tarot of the Witches.

By the time I was 14, I was reading cards at school fetes and doing astrology charts.

...and The Hanged Man

It is interesting to note that more people seem to fear The Hanged Man when it appears in their reading than they do the Death card. It seems almost ingrained in those who come to me for a Tarot reading that death is a new cycle and a death of the past. When The Hanged Man appears they tend to look worried, especially if it shows up in a future position. I think a lot of this is down to the card's link with Judas, and the way that traditionally traitors were hung in Italy.

But on a positive side, the card has a link with Odin, hanging upside down for nine days to achieve wisdom.

To me the presence of The Hanged Man shows a need for evaluation, self-analysis and review. It is often a card of self-sacrifice and indicates someone who puts others before themselves. It is a card that tells you to look at a situation from a different angle, to think carefully and be prepared to change your views.

When The Hanged Man appears in a reading, you will feel you are in a state of suspension and that things seem to be moving very slowly. You can allow yourself to become frustrated by this or you can use the time wisely. By not resisting, that which has eluded you will become clear, and you will find solutions to your problems. Time will be needed to rest and reflect. You may need to rethink priorities and put the needs of others above your own. This may require some sacrifices from you. Answers to your problems are not always obvious and you will gain clarity after a period of deep thought.

⌢

TIFFANY CROSARA

talks Tarot...

―――⌒⌒⌒―――

I first laid my eyes on Tarot, at the tender age of four.
I came across Alfred Douglas's deck, lying on the floor.

The vibrant images of The Star, The Fool, The Magician,
The High Priestess captured my soul, no escaping from
this vision.

And I didn't want to...

I remember that first meeting, like it was yesterday.
I fell in love. It was the start.
This beautiful relationship was here to stay.

Not an easy relationship, but nevertheless, it's stood the
test of time.
This relationship showed my shadow, the shadow became
mine.

It brought vibrant magic, right into my life.
Testing my mental strength, now sharper than a knife.

Teaching me the importance, of balance and respect.
The power of the unconscious, is one I can't reject.

It told me the truth, and tested my ability,
to accept it as it was. Incredible sensibility.

Whenever I needed it, I knew that it was there.
Through independence and codependence, it kept me oh
so aware.

It taught me if we always look, to the external factors,
we will remain oh so empty, as this is no refractor.

But if we look and view, these external factors,
through a mirror of ourselves, we become empowered.
Freeing us from being living re-enactors...

...and The Hanged Man

'I am a control freak who gets haunted by The Hanged Man.'

The Hanged Man made his presence felt in my life during the publication of my first book, *The Transformational Truth of Tarot.*

Not only was he popping up in my readings, but out of them too. The publishers my agent put me in touch with actually appeared to me as walking Hanged Men. The Hanged Man would come up in their readings too. One even proclaimed, 'That's me!'

'I know!' I groaned.

I went to The Witch Museum in Boscastle, Cornwall, where there is a Tarot machine you put a penny in and the dial lands on a Major Arcana – yep, you guessed it!

I attracted a busker that would hang himself upside down near my place of work in Covent Garden!

After 18 months of delays and being stalked by The Hanged Man, I finally turned round and faced him in a meditation, saying, 'Right, I have had enough, I'm ready to hear it, what is it?'

'Tiffany, you are so hung up on the timing of this book – but it is not yours. We gifted it to you, through you. You are but the keeper, not the owner. What gives you the right to determine the timing?'

Wow. What a karmic slap for a Leo!

'Okay!' I said, 'I give it completely over to you then!'

And I let go...

That moment felt like The Star. It was such a blissful feeling to be able to let go of control and hand everything over to the Universe. Yes, even for a Leo!

That very afternoon I had an email from the publisher – received at the time of the meditation – advising a publication date of 31st August. This was the month Spirit had told me my book would be published all along!

~

PHILIP CARR-GOMM

talks Tarot...

M y first meeting with Tarot was in a flat in Notting Hill Gate over 40 years ago. It was the hippy era and a dozen or so of us were gathered in the usual 'sacred circle', passing the peace pipe, and generally basking in the innocence of those times.

One of the company began talking about Tarot, and as he did, he scattered a deck across the floor and started picking out cards at random. He talked about their meaning, sometimes relating them to a person in the circle. I was amazed, and purchased a Rider Waite deck, which I used on and off for the next 30 or so years.

As I studied the Western Mystery Tradition, Tarot, like the Kabbalah, was always there as a useful reference point. But I found I consulted Tarot only occasionally, even though when living in Haiti, we had a big chest made, carved with the image of The Fool dancing above an equal-armed cross encompassed in a circle.

The chest is here in Lewes now, and when Stephanie and I were asked to create The DruidCraft Tarot, I looked at it and smiled. At one end of the chest a Druid is carved, and at the other, a Druidess. The idea that Druidry and Tarot could be connected had at first seemed absurd to me – until we realized that Druidry and Wicca are of course integral parts of the Western Mystery Tradition, and that Tarot offers the ideal medium for illuminating both these ways.

...and Death

Stephanie and I in particular love the image painted by Will Worthington for The DruidCraft Tarot, Arcana XIII, Death. Will has painted not a corny old skeleton with a scythe on a horse, but a loving crone cradling a skull, which she is about to place in the cauldron of rebirth as dawn approaches on the horizon. Part of the section in our book on the interpretation of this card reads: 'We fear death but deep down we know it is needed for change, transformation and rebirth. The wise welcome the cleansing power of this card, which can suggest a time when you will have the opportunity to let go of something that is holding you back.'

At the heart of death is pure compassion. We die to our old selves, old jobs, relationships, homes and battles, so that we can be reborn to new ways of working, living and relating in the world.

Finding this card in a reading suggests you may be at such a moment of initiation – for the core structure of initiation involves an experience of death followed by an experience of rebirth. But we often resist dying, and this is where love and passion can serve a purpose. A powerful love affair or intense erotic passion can seem to split us open and help us to die to our ego or to rigid structures in our personality that we need to abandon. There is a deep mystery in the connection between death and sexuality, as our culture's obsession with these two themes shows. But we need to go deeper than conventional portrayals of these themes to understand their relationship.

Across the circle of the year from Samhain – the Druid and Wiccan festival of death – is Beltane, the festival of spring and of sexuality. We die as a result of being born, and we are born as a result of the sexual urge. The two are inextricably linked, and a passionate erotic relationship – if experienced with spiritual understanding – can lead to a series of initiations in which mask after mask, defence mechanism after defence mechanism, is dropped – or dies – so that the light of the Spirit can shine through. In the end, the lovers experience themselves as divine beings – two aspects of one reality merged in bliss.

This represents one level of meaning and symbolism in the Wiccan Great Rite, and we can see this process of union followed by death, which is followed by rebirth, depicted in the cards when they are laid out in three rows of seven, leaving The Fool apart. The Lovers unite, while below them the Death card appears – through their passion and their love they have died to their outer personalities. Finally below Death comes Rebirth. The new self is born.

The message of this card is: 'The old and unnecessary wants to die. What passion! The new prepares to open like a rosebud at the dawn of a new day.'

LIZ DEAN

talks Death

Death. I'll say it again: Death. Aha! I knew it. I'm sighing with sheer relief and wearing a weak smile of recognition. It's transition time at last, and the skeleton depicted on Death, the card of Scorpio, is brandishing his scythe to clear the metaphorical clutter. He'll banish unsupportive friends and lovers, unfulfilling work and all things outdated, making space for the new. While he's getting busy, we might need, also, to confront what has kept us stuck – from habit to guilt, fear to stubbornness.

But don't dwell too long. Let go, Death says – I'm in charge here, not you. There are higher forces at work, and Death is our opportunity for reconnection and a rebirthing of who we are in the world. It's long overdue; with Death, the cosmos decides enough is enough. Time's up! And of course, Death is the great equalizer: in the Rider Waite deck, the armoured skeleton is triumphant over people of all ranks, from the bishop to the commoner. Materialism and status don't matter in Death's domain, so whatever we may have invested in a situation, emotionally or financially, has no bearing now.

Death's number, unlucky 13, is also uncompromising in its status as a prime number, and marks a turning point in the Major Arcana sequence. From The Fool to the Wheel of Fortune we're on our earthly journey; at XI, Justice, and XII, The Hanged Man, our perspective shifts, sacrifices are made and we move towards the spiritual transformation of Death at XIII, when we can travel into the realms of higher consciousness. We're growing up, and there is a lot to learn along the way.

After Death, we meet Temperance in the form of an angel; then The Devil comes to tempt us before The Tower looms, where our earthly ego and clinging to material matters must finally collapse. Soon we're in the territory of the cosmos itself with The Star, The Moon and The Sun, before Judgement, our ascension to The World and our return to 0, The Fool. Exhausted or overwhelmed already? It's all down to Death – he's offered us a whole new way of living.

Given the richness of Death's symbolism, he has appeared in many guises over the course of Tarot's history, and some are worth a particular mention. The Animal Wisdom Tarot's Moth has a tiny grinning skull embedded in its thorax; the Transition card in the super-sized Sirian Starseed Tarot shows a spirit moving towards the light; The Quantum Tarot's Death has two skeletons in a 'face off' before one becomes antimatter. In my Art of Tarot, Death has a simple sunset and sapling to symbolize old and new. Lisa Hunt's Fairy Tale Tarot offers Beauty attending a dying Beast, with their two faces as lovers in the sky above; The Mythic Tarot shows Death as Hades, the Underworld. Possibly the oldest Tarot, the Visconti-Sforza, has an unnumbered Death who is a skeleton-archer, showing that – like Cupid – Death strikes at random.

Grim Reaper? No. Looking at all these miraculous Deaths, I'm still smiling.

LAURENT LANGLAIS

talks Tarot...

~~~

My Tarot journey started at the age of 16. My mum – a psychic – was deeply involved at the time in learning numerology. She recognized that I, too, was gifted and she started to teach me. I was hooked!

I have given readings ever since, and I have also learned Chinese metaphysics in Asia. I see esotericism as a way to help us fulfil our destinies and make our lives less mundane.

...and Death

I love the Death card and its cathartic effects. Death does not represent the end, but the promise of a new beginning. Death is not the last of the Major Arcana, which clearly indicates that it is a door leading to a new cycle and rebirth.

Without this card, none of the others would have meaning and nothing in our life would have value.

As a Buddhist I welcome these endless opportunities to start anew and evolve.

~~

TRUDY ASHPLANT

talks Tarot...

The flames of the living-room fire flickered. Muted lamplight created ambient shadows on the walls and the fairy lights twinkled their radiant colours. Choristers' heavenly voices flowed out of the TV speakers; all was well that Christmas Eve night. As the clock struck midnight, giving way to the blessed morn, my husband and I began the annual ritual of opening our presents, one by one.

'Look at this... Thank you so much... Not another!' Until only my surprise gift from him remained. This exchange of gifts is one of my favourite parts of the whole festive season, as my husband has never failed to surprise me. On this particular occasion, he surpassed himself!

My fingers carefully unravelled his notoriously bad attempt at wrapping to reveal a deck of Tarot cards. What on earth? Why? My mind raced; I'd never even thought of them, let alone hinted. I was a trained astrologer, yes, but Tarot?

My shock was palpable, but he assured me they would prove to be the best present he had ever bought me.

And so it was on that frosty Christmas morning in the early 90s that my Tarot journey began, leading me from disbelief to fascination, granting me knowledge and ultimately wisdom. My quest continues.

...and Temperance

When I attended my very first Tarot course as a complete beginner, the tutor asked us to select a Major Arcana card. I chose Temperance, purely because I liked the image in The Mythic Tarot I then owned. We were instructed to lie down with our chosen card on our third eye chakra. I was immediately whisked off on a spiritual journey where I became the angel in the card.

I was dancing in a meadow with a sense of profound freedom, knowing that everything in the world was just as it should be. Every action, thought and emotion was spiritually orchestrated; all was well. I recall feeling so light, so trusting, knowing that I could call upon divine guidance at any time. And there were people standing on the edge of the meadow watching me, waiting to ask me for guidance. I knew they were simply waiting their turn to feel like I did.

The bliss and enlightenment I felt was so profound that it has never left me, and is a source of comfort when times get tough.

Surely this is the essence of Temperance? A heavenly reminder that we are all spiritual – we just need to remember to wear this guise on the outside from time to time.

DIANE EBECK

talks Tarot...

It was a massive citrine geode in the window that did it! I stopped, stared and thought, Ooh, who is moving in to the shop next door to my bakery? I like to think it was no coincidence that Kim Arnold opened her shop next door to mine, and it wasn't long before I became intrigued by Kim's passion for Tarot.

As a practicing medium and healer, I was aware of Tarot but had never studied the cards. Under Kim's guidance, I chose my deck, signed up for one of her workshops, and was hooked!

Once I had a taste, I wanted to know more, and I am still learning today. I can't imagine life without my cards. So I thank Kim, for sharing her Tarot skills with me.

I remember when Kim first had the idea for a gathering of Tarot enthusiasts, which became the UK Tarot Conference. I watched her make it a reality and a resounding success. I am so proud to have been there from the beginning and to be watching her celebrate 10 years later.

I want to mention my 'Card of Doom' – The Five of Pentacles. It became a joke between Kim and I that a reading was not complete without this card rearing its head. Kim could see the light shining out from the window, but all I could see was my feet frozen in the snow. Over the years I began to appreciate the lessons and challenges of this card. It is a potent card for the self-employed, but one that teaches us about turning negatives into positives – often a difficult lesson. In time I could see how the card belonged in my readings and I was able to understand its truth. The good news is that I don't see it so often nowadays!

I bought that citrine geode and still have it!

...and Temperance

I have always liked Temperance; its deep symbolism in the Rider Waite deck fascinated me from the start. I find comfort and reassurance in the angelic presence. Living by the sea, I like to put my foot in the water just as Temperance does.

If I am reading for myself, this card reminds me to calm down and go with the flow – not always easy.

For me, Temperance has a special healing energy. I love to meditate on this card; it always makes me feel better.

PAUL HUGHES-BARLOW

talks Tarot...

Tarot was never part of my upbringing, despite purchasing a deck when I was 14. Decks were hard to find in Essex at that time and I quickly put it aside when I did not understand the instructions. Meditation and yoga were my driving forces as a teenager – how could Tarot be part of that? Even when I met my teacher, Punditt Maharaj, and he tricked me into reading palms, I had no interest in Tarot. It was not until I realized that I needed more than palms to do readings that I took an interest.

The day after I purchased my IJJ Swiss Tarot – and with a vague idea of what The Lovers, Death, The Chariot and a few other 'obvious' cards meant – I decided that I was a professional Tarot reader! Between readings I would desperately swot up. I had quickly given up on the Celtic Cross spread and switched to various astrology spreads, which seemed to work well for me.

After one particularly successful Tarot reading – where the client had acknowledged my accuracy and insight – I decided to double-check the meanings of the cards before me. I was shocked to discover that my interpretation had been 'wrong' on every card.

After a prolonged search I discovered Elemental Dignities, which lead to the Golden Dawn system of Tarot, and thence to Crowley's Thoth Tarot.

Although I was no longer resistant to using Tarot, using the Golden Dawn techniques was problematic. One day I bit the bullet, and I laid out an Opening of the Key spread using all five stages. It was months before I got over the trauma.

Even though I could not use it, that spread would not go away, and at some point I began to deconstruct the system. My breakthrough was to interpret cards in groups of three using Elemental Dignities. I was inspired!

By now the internet had become accessible to the public, and I trawled the Tarot news-groups for anything on the Opening of the Key spread – but found nothing. This is how supertarot. co.uk started. Soon a publisher contacted me, and *The Tarot and the Magus* was the result.

My inspiration continues to be the Opening of the Key spread, and Aleister Crowley's Thoth Tarot, which hides a profoundly deep system of spiritual and magical knowledge and challenges me daily.

...and The Devil

The Judeo-Christian gut reaction to The Devil exemplifies the irrational fear of this card. A good Christian would never have a Tarot reading, and a Tarot reader therefore cannot be Christian. Children are told the bogeyman will get them if they do not behave and Christianity instils the same fear, treating us as children. Tarot readers, whether they be New Age or Pagan, still buy into it. How childish.

A petite middle-aged French woman wearing a twin-set, pearls and horn-rimmed glasses once came to me for a reading. She wanted to know about a man she had recently met. Her delicateness prevented me from launching into one of my discussions on sex. As the reading ended, she asked if she could pick one card. She turned over The Devil.

'What does this mean?' she asked.

The word slipped out. 'Bondage,' I replied.

'Ooh!' she said. She had a faraway, misty look in her eyes and went away, seemingly satisfied.

It is our belief in right and wrong that binds us. What if right and wrong were interesting points of view? There would be no resistance or reaction. We would be free.

The Hebrew letter ayin associated with this card means an eye. The eye sees, the mind judges. The mind is so powerful that it can dictate or invent what the eye sees. The eye makes no judgement on what it sees. To not see is surely the greatest sin. The Gematria value of AYN is 61, which relates to Nothing, and ANY the Self.

Far from representing gross materialism – the lowest, most degraded aspect of life – this card points to the highest knowledge of the Self as Nothing, which projects and sees everything as All. To achieve this, Capricorn is firmly fixed on the goal – not gross materialism, but something far higher, the goal of Samadhi.

More than any other card, The Devil represents the liberation of the mind to achieve inner peace.

᷒

CHLOE McCRACKEN

talks Tarot...

It feels like Tarot has always been in my life. In the late 70s, my mother read with an original Rider Waite that she kept wrapped in a silk scarf in a wooden box. As teens in the 80s, my best friend and I read the cards, asking about boys and parents, friends and school. In my 20s, my partner was into Crowley and the Thoth, a passion I never joined him in! In my 30s I moved to Madrid, and my best friend was a witch who read Tarot and also introduced me to Wicca, runes and angel cards.

When I moved back to London I decided to learn more about Tarot for myself, and took a beginner's course at Mysteries in Covent Garden.

I discovered the Aeclectic Tarot Forum and the Tarot Association of the British Isles. I discovered Lenormand's, in the form of Titania's Fortune Cards.

Since then the cards have become both a job and a passion for me, and something I can't imagine living without. I've done readings face to face, by email and SMS, and spent nearly a year working for a psychic phone line.

These days, I'm more likely to be found blogging, teaching or working on deck ideas. The Celtic Lenormand will be published by US Games in 2014, and I have a couple of other projects in the pipeline...

...and The Tower

The Tower is a card that people, myself included, are rarely happy to see come up in a reading. And yet, like all 78 cards, it has both positive and negative aspects and isn't just black or white. One of the first decks I bought, the Osho Zen Tarot, described The Tower as: 'A shake-up that's a wake-up!' As sound bites go, I think it represents The Tower pretty well.

On the one hand, we have the side of The Tower that represents a shock, often coming out of the blue. Something that shatters our sense of self or rocks our foundations. It may be something we could have foreseen, but more often than not we don't. For example, people emigrate for many reasons, perhaps from fear of death at the hands of political enemies, or from a desire to have a better life. And yet, whether it is something we choose gladly or not, it is still hard to really understand all the changes that such a move will bring. Losing home, family, friends, jobs, language and qualifications are factors that can affect us in ways we don't expect, even if we were looking forward to the move.

On the other hand – after the destruction – there is the potential for new growth, for rebuilding something better. Whether the old is completely destroyed, or whether we simply have to adjust our way of being, there are always new possibilities called forth by change.

Another aspect of this card is in the question: How much of this shake-up is because of our set patterns of action or thought?

Is it our clinging to the old that actually causes the problem, rather than the 'shocking' event?

Ultimately, time often shows us that what seemed like destruction was actually simply change, neither good nor bad. Once we can let go of our old sense of self, we can embrace the new possibilities that open up when one door closes.

Overall, I believe releasing is easier when we have chosen the change ourselves rather than when it is forced on us. And strangely, it can be easier when the change is large rather than subtle, as then we can at least see what we are facing.

I can't say that I've come to love Tower experiences, but I am learning to embrace them.

SUZANNE CORBIE

talks Tarot...

I was 16 when I was first shown Tarot and those fascinating images were just too enchanting to leave alone. I found myself gazing at them, questioning them and dreaming of them. There were not so many books back then and they did not reveal as much as modern books do. And yet, they hinted at depths of wisdom without saying. They fascinated me.

I lingered on the cards. I meditated on them, questioned them, entered their realms and they taught me. The Fool encouraged me to leap; The Magician taught me how to create a story; The High Priestess revealed her mystery – but only when I asked the right questions; The Empress wrapped her loving arms around me and spoke to me of love – its pain, its suffering and its power to transform. The Emperor schooled me in responsibility and dedication, and The Hierophant in developing a code of morals and ethics. The Lovers came and went, until I learned understanding; The Chariot urged me forward when my motivation waned; Strength was with me all along, if only I had realized; and The Hermit took time to appreciate, but he was so worth the wait.

The Wheel of Fortune turned and I spent time swinging in the wind with The Hanged Man – letting go seems like the hardest thing in the world and yet when you feel the breeze of freedom through your limbs, there is no better feeling. Sometimes I dispensed Justice and other times I received it. Death came and went, leaving its presence in my heart – it is an old friend now. Temperance was always a healing balm in my soul between The Devil and The Tower, holding sway over me. I have no fear of them any more and even smile when I see them. The Star, The Sun and The Moon – in turn – inspired confidence, humanity and an ability to see in the dark, and as Judgement released me, I became whole and The World became my oyster.

Now, many years later, I have gone back to the beginning. Seeing Tarot as if for the first time, learning from teachers skilled in areas I hadn't previously been aware of, studying the mysterious story of Tarot and even travelling to see old cards and old places where it originated. My journey has only just begun – what about yours?

...and The Tower

I am very fond of Arcana XVI – The Tower. I know some will think that's crazy – what is there to like about it? It's all about destruction, annihilation and devastation. Why like that card when you have the vision of The Star and the beauty of The Empress to compare it with?

And how many of us cringe at the sight of it in a reading? Either it's going to shake up our own little lives or we may have difficulty explaining it to a client, especially if they take one look at it and say, 'Ooh, don't like the look of that one!'

But shake up our lives it does, and how wonderfully liberating that can be. Stuck in our ivory towers of judgement and our long-standing patterns of familiarity and ignorance, it takes the powerful energy of Mars to question that judgement, and to shake our foundations to the core with the lightning bolt of clarity and truth. The wisdom of the higher self unseats the material self from its throne, and its crown comes crashing down.

And how incredibly relevant is that to this time and this age? We are collectively living out The Tower card as established structures of greed and power are exposed over and over again, their towers tumbling down around us. And the next card in the Major Arcana sequence – The Star – offers us a way forward that is based on honesty, connecting with our communities, working together for the greater good and taking care of the world around us – if we choose to learn the lesson and have the courage to let go of that which is familiar for a new beginning.

The Hebrew letter peh – with which The Tower is connected – refers to the mouth and the powers of speech, reminding us of the power of words and their effect on others. What we say, what we don't say, what we call ourselves and others. What we provoke through our words, our vows, our promises and whether we keep them – these all have a power that shapes our lives and the lives of those around us. Thinking about what we communicate can change everything in a heartbeat and bring our towers crashing down.

If our tower is not built on sure foundations, then the clarity of the lightning bolt is its greatest gift – treasure it.

⌒

JANE STRUTHERS
talks Tarot...

$\sim\!\infty\!\sim$

Tarot found me when I was 14, through the pages of *19* magazine. The centre spread of one edition was devoted to illustrations of the Major Arcana taken from the Rider Waite deck. I knew almost nothing about Tarot but the images looked intriguing and I glued them on to the backs of cereal packets. It took quite a while to complete the set. The cards worked fairly well but I soon replaced them with a Marseilles deck. It was wonderful to have the entire 78 cards instead of just 22, but that pleasure was outweighed by the difficulty of using the Minor Arcana. What on earth did all those cards signify and how would I ever remember their meanings?

In the early 70s in Eastbourne, it was hard to find any books on Tarot, astrology, palmistry and all the other subjects that fascinated me. My only option was to spend hours in second-hand bookshops, where I found an intriguing selection of titles on everything from astral travel to how to read playing cards. The books were all years old and often frustratingly short on detail. But for all their shortcomings, they gave me the thrilling sense of being able to tap into another world – one that promised insight into what was going on around me and what would happen in the future.

I discovered Alfred Douglas's book, *The Tarot*. It was a beacon shining in the darkness. I was still struggling with my Marseilles deck, which, I must admit, I never grew to like. Years later, I solved my problem by buying a Rider Waite deck, and finally began to grasp the many meanings of the Minor Arcana.

...and The Sun

I always smile when I turn up this card. It's so joyful and vibrant, and has a warmth I can almost feel beating down on me. I love its interesting detail, especially in the Rider Waite deck where four sunflowers are in bloom above a stone wall, with the sun behind them.

Sunflowers are heliotropic when in bud and track the sun across the sky. Perhaps the symbolism – with the sunflowers facing away from the sun – is suggesting that each of us contains a divine spark and a creative impulse that we shouldn't ignore or underestimate. We all have something unique to offer the world.

This card carries very happy memories for me as I associate it with my older niece. It predicted her conception at a time when that seemed highly unlikely.

I gave my brother a reading at the kitchen table on Christmas night in 1996. We were staying with my mother and as I didn't have a proper deck with me, I had to cobble one together using my first set of Major Arcana cards – still in a drawer in my old bedroom – and an ordinary pack of playing cards. This of course meant the deck consisted of cards of two different sizes and was missing the four knights. It was imperfect but workable.

I dealt out a simple twelve-card spread, with one card representing each month of the coming year. The spread talked about many things, including my brother's work. But the card for April was The Sun, and to me it was shouting one thing and one thing only: the conception of a child. Normally, I wouldn't dream of saying something so specific, especially given a child was so longed for, but I just blurted it out. The card for December was the 10 of Cups, which I took as confirmation of the child's birth. Sure enough, that is exactly what happened. My niece was born almost twelve months to the day after that kitchen-table Tarot reading.

❧

MAJOR TOM SCHICK

talks Tarot...

When I was 10 years old my family went down to the bus station to pick up a cousin who was coming to visit. Dressed in torn, faded jeans and a dirty mackintosh, Tarot approached me and offered me a piece of candy. My father took Tarot aside and told it off in no uncertain terms. I didn't get any candy!

As a young child I learned about divination from my grandmother's reading of tea leaves. In my teens, I attended a spiritualist Christian church, where I learned psychometry and colour healing. I didn't really learn to read the cards until I started reading for drinks in the various 'titty' bars surrounding the swamps of northern Louisiana in my early 20s. I was a lieutenant in the US Air Force at the time.

In 2002 I decided to make Tarot my profession and focused my efforts on education, creative expression and personal development. I have since given workshops in Dallas, Las Vegas, London, Melbourne, San Francisco and New York.

Inspired by creative individual imagination expressed in Tarot cards, I edit and publish the *Tarot Lovers' Calendar*.

In 2005, The Association for Tarot Studies printed a limited edition of my Tarot of Marseilles to commemorate the

Melbourne International Tarot Conference. Schiffer Publishing published a second edition in 2007 and it is still widely available.

...and The Sun

I have difficulty pointing to one Tarot card and saying, that's my favourite! I love all the cards. Tomorrow it may be The Moon or Judgement. Next week, Death or The Devil. Right now I rather like The Sun.

There's a long-standing duality in pictorial representation of The Sun that has fractured like shards of glass in more modern versions. We have the ubiquitous sun with a face. Then we either see a figure on horseback with a banner, or we see a pair of children together on the grass. This iconography is as old as the Tarot of Marseilles and its contemporaries the Viéville, Bodet and Vandenborre.

The original iconography – from the Visconti decks – of a child holding aloft a red sun bearing a recognizable human face, has almost entirely disappeared.

Since the 70s the iconography used to depict The Sun has exploded, with practically as many symbols as there are artists who employ them. In some decks direct depiction of the sun itself has disappeared, and we are treated to symbolic representations such as sunflowers, gold coins, a beach, birds flying and so on.

This iconography inevitably determines how one interprets the card, no matter what the setting. One could further argue that without setting, no interpretation is possible. Without context, one can only give clues to meaning.

I rather like what Paul Foster Case wrote in his book *The Tarot: A Key to the Wisdom of the Ages*, regarding two children:

'This Key represents the fifth stage of unfoldment.... For though it is a stage wherein all physical forces are under the control of the adept, who, having himself become childlike, realizes in his own person the fulfilment of the promise, "A little child shall lead them" – yet a person who has reached this grade still feels himself to be a separate, or at least a distinct entity.'

Of the symbol of the child on horseback, Case says:

'He is the regenerated personality, recognizing and affirming its unity with the Father, or Source of all. He leaves behind the artificial erections of race-consciousness, and fares forth free and joyous on his journey home.'

Thus we begin to see where The Sun's associations with happiness, joy and innocence have come from. But for goodness' sake, don't forget that The Sun can fry your carcass to a crisp.

⌒

MELANIE YOUNG

talks Tarot...

~~~

I can't actually remember how my Tarot journey began, but I do recall being fascinated by ghost stories as a child. I used to read a lot and would creep into the adult section of my local library. I spent hours absorbed in books, fascinated by esoteric subjects.

Despite having attended a Catholic school where Tarot, astrology and the like were frowned upon, I wanted to find out more.

I first met Kim Arnold at a workshop she was running, and I would often go into her shop in Birchington. She introduced me to Tarot and I was like a sponge, soaking up this new and exciting information. A different world had opened up for me.

The workshops run by the Psychic Café allowed me to explore esoteric subjects in depth and meet like-minded people. I discovered that Tarot spreads were a powerful means for self-exploration and growth. I began to use Tarot for spiritual development, meditation and contemplation. Now, whenever I have a problem or I'm struggling with something in my life, I consult the cards.

In 2003 I went to the first Tarot Conference at The London Art House, and 10 years on, having been involved with them all, I am still learning about Tarot. I'm not sure you ever stop.

...and The Star

The Star is confirmation that you are on the right path and should not let anyone hurry you along or put you off. Everything occurs with perfect timing.

Follow the path that makes you happy and leads to enlightenment and fulfilment. Accept your faults and love yourself in spite of them.

The Star brings hope, optimism and peace. When we have hope, we have something to live for and somewhere to move towards. It is a healing card and reminds us to look after ourselves and have faith in the future. It is a light at the end of the tunnel. The Star reminds us not to dwell on negative thoughts but to keep our energy positive.

Follow your dreams, but remember that the dreams most likely to come true are the ones we make happen through our own efforts. We all have our own inner Star and it is up to us to nurture it so we can sparkle.

꒰꒱

THE CONTRIBUTORS

RICHARD ABBOT learned about the unseen dimensions of life over a 20-year study period with Arthur Norris. He uses a wide variety of mystic arts and psychic skills – focused around his unique application of Tarot and Numerology – as tools for self-discovery, empowerment and growth, as well as providing healing for those in pain. He has written numerous books and courses, and has appeared at events in the UK and the USA. His work is innovative and offers the chance of deep transformation for all sincere seekers. The Hermitage Development Centre, where Richard trained, was originally established in 1983 by Arthur Norris and Pat Warrington, and now continues under Richard's guidance. **www.yourwayforward.co.uk**

TRUDY ASHPLANT is a clairvoyant Tarot Reader and Spiritual Teacher living in Durham, UK. She specializes in teaching the Tarot from beginner to professional level. She is a certified Angel and Ascension Teacher, BAPS Consultant, and is Angelic Reiki attuned. 'My passion is your spiritual growth. To see you connect with and move forward on your path. My guides are my teachers, just as I may be yours right now. But I believe that we are all both student and teacher, and that we learn from one another. The greatest return I receive is witnessing people take a step forward on their path.' **www.trudyjashplant.co.uk**

GERALDINE BESKIN has a lifelong interest in Western Esotericism. She and her daughter Bali run the UK's oldest occult shop, The Atlantis Bookshop. Geraldine is interested in most aspects of the Western Mysteries and is passionate about the personalities who were involved with them, and tries to keep those great names alive through her biographical talks. Geraldine has been a supporter of the UK Tarot Conference since it began. **www.theatlantisbookshop.com**

PHILIP CARR-GOMM is a psychologist and author of many books on spirituality, including *Sacred Places* and *Druid Craft: The Magic of Wicca and Druidry*. For the last 25 years he has been the leader of the world's largest Druid group, the Order of Bards Ovates and Druids, which has over 15,000 members. Their training course is published in seven languages, and their monthly podcast reaches 20,000 listeners a month. Philip and Stephanie Carr-Gomm have created The Druid Animal Oracle, The Druid Plant Oracle and The Druid Craft Tarot, all illustrated by Will Worthington. These are now available as iPhone apps, as well conventional decks with accompanying manuals. **www.philipcarrgomm.druidry.org**

CILLA CONWAY is the author of *The Intuitive Tarot* and *The Devas of Creation*. Cilla is an intuitive artist who works primarily with the concept of alchemy and archetypal energies. **www.cillaconway.com**

SUZANNE CORBIE has long been involved in mystical spiritual traditions. She studied Tarot primarily as a tool for inner wisdom, and weaves together her knowledge, experience and intuitive understanding to inspire students around the world. For the last 14 years, she has read professionally and taught Tarot courses and workshops in London and the south east, as well as lecturing and teaching at the Mystic Arts Festival, Mind Body and Soul Experience, the UK Tarot Conference and The Victoria and Albert and Tate Modern Museums in London. Her *Goddess Workshop* CD (Paradise Music) has proved an immensely popular learning tool for Tarot students globally. **www.suzannecorbie.co.uk**

TIFFANY CROSARA began her psychic and Tarot journey aged four. In her early twenties she immersed herself in psychic studies, and at 26 she opened her own centre and began reading professionally and teaching. Tiffany went on to read for well-known organizations, including Mysteries in London's Covent Garden, and taught alongside top names in today's Tarot and Mind, Body, Spirit field. Tiffany's first book, *The Transformational Truth of Tarot*, won an award for best spiritual book of 2012. Tiffany now performs readings on live TV. **www.tiffanycrosara.com**

ALISON CROSS is a Tarotist and writer who concentrates on making the Tarot's Court Cards more fun and easy to understand. A former Chairman of the Tarot Association of The British Isles and Editor of TABI's quarterly e-zine, Alison has contributed articles and reviews to publications as diverse as *The Times* and *Prediction* magazine. She also delivers monthly Tarot workshops for the Glasgow Tarot Meetup Group. Alison broadcasts a weekly internet radio show on Radio Bute which includes a Tarot reading for one lucky listener. She lives on the Scottish island of Bute with her partner and son. **www.tarot-thrones.blogspot.co.uk**

INA CÜSTERS-VAN BERGEN is a Dutch Magistra, Occultist, Mystic, Reiki Master, spiritual coach and international author. She is the founder and Director of Studies of the first internationally recognized school for applied hermetics in the Netherlands: the Hermetic Order of the Temple of Starlight. The school has a direct lineage to the Golden Dawn, via Dion Fortune, Ernest Butler and Dolores Ashcroft-Nowicki. Ina uses the ancient Egyptian maxim 'Unifying the Two Lands' as her magical motto because it summarizes the work of the Magister: connecting the spiritual and material realities. **www.templeofstarlight.eu**

LIZ DEAN is the author of five successful Tarot/divination decks and books: Fairy Tale Fortune Cards, The Golden Tarot, The Mystery of the Tarot, The Love Tarot and the international bestseller, The Art of Tarot. For two years, she co-edited *Kindred Spirit*, the UK's leading spiritual magazine. Liz is a publishing consultant for Octopus Publishing, overseeing the Godsfield and Gaia lists of mind, body, spirit books, and reads Tarot professionally at Selfridges, London. She has been a speaker at The UK Tarot Conference and founded with Kay Stopforth The London Tarot Salon, a workshop series that focused on Tarot archetypes as illuminations of the creative process. Liz has been researching and reading Tarot cards for almost 25 years; she bought her first deck, the Morgan Greer, in 1989. **www.lizdean.com** and **www.mrsnorth.com**

ALFRED DOUGLAS studied monthly articles on the Tarot written by the occultist Madeline Montalban in the late 50s. In 1961 he joined her correspondence school and continued to study Tarot until meeting his wife (the writer and astrologer Jo Sheridan) in 1967. Alfred's book on the I Ching was published in 1971, and his second book, *The Tarot: The Origins, Meaning and Uses of the Cards* was published in 1972 with a new deck of 78 Tarot cards drawn by David Sheridan. It stayed in print for over 30 years, and Alfred republished both book and cards in 2006. Alfred now also runs Madeline's esoteric school, the Order of the Morning Star. **www.sheridandouglas.co.uk**

DIANE EBECK is a medium, spiritual healer, hypnotherapist, Reiki Master and Tarot reader. She has been involved with the UK Tarot Conference since it began in 2003, working as right-hand woman to Kim Arnold, the founder and organizer. Diane is a professional Tarot reader and continues to study the Tarot, seeking further guidance and knowledge.

SASHA FENTON became a professional astrologer, palmist and Tarot reader in 1973, but her readings tailed off in the late 1980s when her writing career took off. She has since written 126 books, with sales of over 6.5 million and translations into 12 languages. Sasha wrote the stars columns for the *Sunday People* and *Woman's Own*, and has contributed to many newspapers, magazines, radio and TV programmes worldwide. Sasha has twice been President of the British Astrological and Psychic Society (BAPS), Chair and Treasurer of The Advisory Panel on Astrological Education and a member of the Executive Council of the Writers' Guild. Sasha now co-manages Zambezi Publishing Ltd. **www.zampub.com**

ADAM FRONTERAS has over 30 years' experience as a Professional Consultant in astrology, Tarot and dream interpretation. He is currently Executive Producer for My Spirit Productions, which creates internet radio for mind, body and spirit programmes. Adam has written a number of books, including *Instant Tarot*, and *The Tarot* (Carlton Books), and has his own column in a number of national magazines. Adam is a regular astrologer and Dream Analyst for a number of TV and radio broadcasters, including BBC Radio, BBC1 Breakfast News and Sky News 24. Adam has monthly shows on BBC Oxford and Foxy Bingo Radio, as well as his own show on My Spirit Radio. **www.adamfronteras.net**

MARY K. GREER is an independent scholar, writer, teacher and professional Tarot consultant. She has an MA in English Literature from the University of Central Florida where she also first taught Tarot in 1974. For 11 years, she taught at New College of California in San Francisco, including Tarot as an interdisciplinary subject integrating art, literature, history, and psychology. She is the author of 10 books on Tarot and on magic, and in 2007 won the International Tarot Lifetime Achievement Award from the Association for Tarot Studies. Mary continues to travel around the world teaching Tarot and the Petit Lenormand deck. She currently produces Mary K. Greer's Tarot Blog at **www.marygreer.wordpress.com**

LINDA HARE (aka Rowan) is a Hedge witch, Tarot reader and teacher. Linda has run many courses and workshops over the years and continues to share her vast knowledge with those wanting to learn more.

LYN HOWARTH-OLDS has been involved in Tarot for many years, enjoying roles as a reader, teacher, mentor and conference presenter. Her focus at present is to unite her love of Tarot with a growing interest in artistic ventures that celebrate the art of Tarot in its many guises. Lyn has been involved in many projects worldwide, including the ATS Convention in St Suzanne, France, and has taken part in the Tarot Art and History tour of Northern Italy. **www.tarot-ART.com**

PAUL HUGHES-BARLOW is a mystic and magician who has specialized in studying spiritual and magickal techniques for developing higher states of consciousness using the Tarot. The fruits of some of this work are found on the Super Tarot website and in his book, *Tarot and the Magus*, which explores divination, magical and spiritual techniques based upon the Golden Dawn methods of the Opening of the Key Spread. As well as writing Book II on the Opening of the Key Spread, which will explore more new methods of interpreting the Tarot, Paul is also working on revelations connecting the Atbash code with the Tarot. **www.supertarot.co.uk**

CORRINE KENNER specializes in bringing metaphysical subjects down to earth. She has written several books, including *Tarot and Astrology, Tarot for Writers, Astrology for Writers*, and *Tarot Journaling*. Corrine is the creator of The Wizards Tarot and The Epicurean Tarot, and the co-creator of The Tarot of Physics. Much of her work has been translated for a worldwide audience. Corrine was raised on a family farm in North Dakota. She studied in Brazil and Los Angeles, where she earned a degree in philosophy from California State University and worked as a newspaper reporter. She currently lives in Minneapolis, Minnesota, with her husband Dan, a software developer, and their four daughters. **www.corrinekenner.com**

LAURENT LANGLAIS is a Feng Shui expert and consultant who works all over the UK and internationally. At a young age, she was initiated into some of the western metaphysics, including numerology and Tarot. Over the years she has learned that there is more to our world than just 'what meets the eye', and that natural and cosmic forces are shaping our fate and happiness. **www.spacessential.com**

JANE LYLE is an astrologer, author, clairvoyant and Tarot reader. She has co-created two Tarot decks, the bestselling Lovers' Tarot and The Renaissance Tarot, which blend astrology with symbolism for practical interpretations. Jane was a consultant and contributing editor on *Zodiac*, a major astrology part-work, and has written for various national newspapers and magazines. Her horoscope columns have appeared in *Scotland on Sunday* and *Cosmo Girl*. Jane has also appeared regularly on radio and TV, and is published in more than 15 languages. **http://theastrologyroom.com/astrologers/jane-lyle**

CIRO MARCHETTI is a British graphic designer whose professional career began in the mid-70s after graduating from Croydon College of Art, UK, and has since included work in Europe, South America and the USA. Ciro has always been a keen illustrator, and over the last few years has started to apply his experience with digital media to produce a number of illustrations. While produced mainly for personal satisfaction, his work has also enjoyed a degree of recognition, having appeared in a number of print and online publications. Ciro has created beautiful Tarot decks that sell internationally. **www.ciromarchetti.com**

CAITLÍN MATTHEWS has written over 50 books on shamanism, myth and spirituality. She teaches all over the world and is recognized as a foremost expert in cartomancy. She has devised four divinatory systems. Her latest project, The Enchanted Lenormand (2013), will be followed by The Lenormand Learner. **www.hallowquest.org.uk**

JOHN MATTHEWS has written over 100 books, mostly in the field of metaphysics, as well as history, myth and folklore. He has devised five Tarot decks and is working on a further three. His latest works are *The Oracle of Dr John Dee* and *Faeryland*. **www.hallowquest.org.uk**

CHLOE McCRACKEN holds a Masters degree in Social Anthropology and is currently completing a Masters in Psychotherapy and Counselling. She has worked as a professional Tarot and oracle reader since 2006, and has been blogging on the subject since 2010. She is the author of the Celtic Lenormand, with artwork by Will Worthington, which is due to be published in 2014 by U.S. Games. **www.innerwhispers.co.uk**

MARK McELROY is a writer and corporate storyteller living in Atlanta, Georgia. He published his first book, *Putting the Tarot to Work*, in 2004. Since then, he's written many Tarot books, including *The Absolute Beginner's Guide to Tarot*, and designed seven Tarot decks, including the Lo Scarabeo Tarot and the Tarot of the Celtic Fairies. He's currently working on *The Best Tarot Book for Beginners Ever Written*, which is due to publish on the 10th anniversary of the publication of his first book. At madebymark.com he writes about world travel, personal technology, spirituality, and life in Midtown Atlanta. Tarot-related posts from madebymark.com are cross-posted to the Facebook group Tarotholics Anonymous. **www.madebymark.com**

RICCARDO MINETTI is an editor for Lo Scarabeo based in Italy. He has contributed to several Lo Scarabeo projects and is the author of the book that accompanies the Fey Tarot. Lo Scarabeo have played a generous part in supporting the UK Tarot Conference. **www.loscarabeo.com**

ADELE NOZEDAR is an author and a professional forager whose abiding interest is in the hidden meanings of things. Her previous books include *The Secret Language of Birds*, from which the Tarot deck of the same name was fledged, the bestselling *Signs and Symbols Sourcebook*, *The Element Encyclopaedia of Native Americans*, *Freaky Dreams* and the bestselling *The Hedgerow Handbook: Remedies, Recipes and Rituals*. **www.adelenozedar.com**

NAOMI OZANIEC has been involved in the Western Mystery tradition since 1975. She was the Oracular Voice of Isis at the World Parliament of Religions in Chicago. Although her main interest is in the spirituality of ancient Egypt, Naomi is an inspirational and original writer; she has written on many aspects of the Western tradition including meditation, Tarot as an initiatory symbol system, Qabalah and the historical role of the priestess. Naomi is passionate about the re-emergence of the Divine Feminine as a vitalizing presence in the creation of a new global vision. Naomi is the founder of The House of Life Mystery School, founded on the mysticism of Ancient Egypt.

CARRIE PARIS MA has a passion for divination, Tarot, and ancient ceremonial rites that invoke the spirit of sacred plants. She is the creator of talkingtarot.com, The Virtual Tarot Classroom and has been in Tarot practice for over 15 years. She heads Santa Fe's two Tarot Meetup groups with a membership of 250, is co-founder and organizer of LETS: Land of Enchantment Tarot Symposium, and was in the first class to receive a Masters degree in the Cultural Study of Cosmology and Divination from the University of Kent, UK. Through the use of the internet and video technology, Carrie now offers her classes and divination services to a global clientele in the USA, Asia and Europe. **www.carrieparis.com**

RACHEL POLLACK is the author of 34 books, including fiction, non-fiction, poetry, translation and art. Her *78 Degrees of Wisdom* has been in print continuously since 1980, and has been described around the world as 'the Bible of Tarot readers'. Rachel has won three awards and her work has been translated into 14 languages. She has taught Tarot in Europe, North America, Australia and New Zealand. Rachel designed and drew the Shining Tribe Tarot deck. Her most recent project is The Burning Serpent Oracle, a Lenormand deck produced in collaboration with world-famous Tarot artist Robert M. Place. Her novel, *The Child Eater*, is due out in 2014. **www.rachelpollack.com**

MARK RYAN has been combining his acting, singing, writing and Action Direction talents in an eclectic and successful international career spanning over 30 years. Mark worked with John Matthews and Will Worthington to create the Wildwood Tarot, an idea based on the Greenwood Tarot he created with Chesca Potter. Mark wrote the book that accompanies the Greenwood Tarot, which is now a highly sought-after and collectable deck. **www.thewildwoodtarot.com**

MAJOR TOM SCHICK edits and publishes the *Tarot Lovers' Calendar*, now in its 12th year. In 2005, The Association of Tarot Studies printed a limited edition Major Tom's Tarot of Marseilles to commemorate the Melbourne International Tarot Conference. Schiffer Publishing subsequently published a second edition in 2007, which is still widely available. Major Tom has presented at Tarot conferences in London, Melbourne, New York, San Francisco and Dallas. **www.majortom.biz**

JULIET SHARMAN-BURKE is an analytic psychotherapist, and has been practicing Tarot and astrology for over 20 years. She is well known as a teacher of Tarot and has written several books on the subject, including *A Beginners Guide to Tarot*, *Understanding the Tarot* and *Mastering the Tarot*. She designed The Sharman-Caseli deck, and co-authored The Mythic Tarot deck and book with Liz Greene. Alongside Juliet's therapy practice, teaching, writing and organizing the Centre for Psychological Astrology in London, Juliet teaches in the USA, Norway, Slovenia and Holland, and gives talks at conferences in the UK. **www.cpalondon.com/juliet.html**

JANE STRUTHERS taught herself Tarot, astrology and palmistry in her teens, little realizing that they would all form an important part of her career. She is a consultant astrologer and Tarot reader, and has lectured on all three topics for the London School of Astrology. She is also a trained healer and is currently training to be a homeopath. Jane is the author of over 30 books on a variety of subjects, from the British countryside to mind, body and spirit. Her books include *The Destiny Tarot, Tarot for Life and Love, Working with Auras, The Psychic's Bible* and *The Wisdom of Trees Oracle*. Jane shares a 17th-century cottage in rural East Sussex with her husband and their two cats. **www.janestruthers.com**

LISA TENZIN-DOLMA is the creator of The Glastonbury Tarot cards and book set, which was first published by Gothic Image in Europe and Weiser Inc. in the USA and Canada. A special deluxe edition has now been published by Papaveria Press. Lisa is the author of 16 books and over 500 articles on a wide variety of subjects. She is a consultant to film-makers, and an ambassador for The Goodwill Treaty which was founded by humanitarian and Nobel Prize nominee Bryant McGill. As a qualified canine behaviour specialist, she is principal of The International School of Canine Practitioners. The central focus in all of Lisa's work is self-motivation, healing, self-understanding and self-empowerment. **www.tenzindolma.co.uk**

MELANIE YOUNG has worked alongside Kim Arnold for over 10 years, and has been a familiar face at the Conference from the very beginning. Amongst her many skills, Melanie is an accomplished Tarot reader and artist.

⌒

ABOUT THE AUTHOR

Kim Arnold is a professional Tarot reader and teacher, and the founder of the prestigious UK Tarot Conference, an event that brings together some of the most exciting names in Tarot from around the world. Her career highlight to date is her packed-out one-woman show at the Barons Court Theatre, London. Called 'Is This It?', Kim's show used the Tarot as a prop for enlightening the audience.

Kim occasionally does consultancy work for Universal Studios. Her most memorable project was working on the 2010 movie *The Wolfman*, in which she helped the actress Geraldine Chaplin prepare for her part, which required her to read the Tarot.

Recently Kim was runner-up in the *Kindred Spirit* Magazine Spiritual Entrepreneur Awards.